The MIRACLE MORNING
for PARENTS & FAMILIES **PLAYBOOK**

THE COMPANION GUIDE TO
THE MIRACLE MORNING FOR PARENTS & FAMILIES

HAL ELROD · MIKE & LINDSAY McCARTHY

WITH HONORÉE CORDER

THE MIRACLE MORNING FOR PARENTS AND FAMILIES PLAYBOOK

Hal Elrod & Honorée Corder

Cover and Interior Design: Dino Marino, www.dinomarino.com

ISBN-978-1-942589-36-5

TABLE OF CONTENTS

INTRODUCTION

The Miracle Morning for Parents and Families was originally released in September of 2016. At the time, Tyler was seven, Ember was three, and Mike and I had just celebrated our ten-year wedding anniversary. We had not been parenting that long and, quite frankly, did not feel qualified to be writing a "parenting" book. To be completely honest, we wrote that book more for ourselves than for anyone else. Toni Morrison said, "If there's a book that you want to read, but it hasn't been written yet, then you must write it." So, that is what we did.

The Miracle Morning for Parents and Families became our family handbook that we just so happened to share with the world. I found as a stay-at-home mom with young children, The Miracle Morning Hal talked about was a little out of reach for me. I didn't always have the luxury of controlling my time in the morning when hungry children were begging for my attention. There wasn't a guidebook about how to make The Miracle Morning a family practice or how to adapt it to children, so we created it.

In writing that book, Mike and I had a lot of discussions about how we wanted to lead our family, how we wanted to show up as parents for our kids, and what qualities we admired in parents we considered to be exceptional. Through those discussions, we came up with what we like to call the "three Ps of parenting." They are Purposefulness, Playfulness, and Perspective. I'm happy to report we have followed our own advice and are constantly developing new visions for our family, defining what we need to do and moving in that direction, tracking our progress, and updating and evolving our approach, which is where this book comes into play.

Here we are, five years after the original release of *The Miracle Morning for Parents and Families*. Tyler is twelve, Ember is eight, and Mike and I just celebrated fifteen years of marriage. We have been spending the last five years traveling, learning, blogging, developing systems for our household, and facilitating family events to teach these systems to other families. We've been through many iterations of these exercises and have done lots of trial and error. We have also taken groups of other families through these exercises with great results, and we finally feel like we can effectively share them with *you*.

Mike and I wrote *The Miracle Morning for Parents and Families* to answer the question, *"Why* do we parent the way we do?" Much of that book was theory. This book, *The Miracle Morning for Parents and Families Playbook*, is all about answering *"How* do we parent the way we do?" After years of experimenting with our theories, they have become actual practices. We'd call this a workbook, but no one likes to do work. Just like a sports team has a playbook of different strategies, your family needs one too. This book will help your family create the systems to win at the game of parenting.

ASKING BETTER QUESTIONS

We may think that as parents, we are supposed to have all the answers, but I think we can hurt our relationship with our children with that thinking. In our experience, it's better to have the right questions than the right answers. In Warren Berger's book, *A More Beautiful Question,* he writes, "In some ways, it can be more difficult or risky for those in authority to question."

In Hal Gregersen's study of business leaders who question, he found that they exhibited an unusual "blend of humility and confidence"—they were humble enough to acknowledge a lack of knowledge and confident enough to admit this in front of others. When we can admit to our kids that we, too, are still learning and even allow them to take the lead sometimes, together, we can create much more creative and beautiful solutions to our everyday issues simply by asking better questions. Most of the exercises in this book are based on an approach called Appreciative Inquiry, which Mike learned through completing the Xchange facilitator training program with our close friend and master facilitator, Jon Berghoff. You can find out more about the program at his website: https://xchangeapproach.com/.

I like www.PositivePsychology.com's definition: "Appreciative Inquiry (AI) is a way to engage groups of people in self-determined change. It focuses on what's working, rather than what's not working, and leads people to co-designing their future." That methodology was created to help businesses solve problems, but when Mike learned about it, he saw great potential for its use in family units. Families, like businesses, are groups of people who need to work together to create solutions to everyday challenges and reach common goals. Many businesses run smoothly because they have defined best practices, checklists, shared values, goals, and consistent processes. This book will help your family create some of those same things to run like a well-oiled machine.

We created this book to help you ask better questions. It's designed to bring the family together to create harmony in your home. The following exercises will help bring clarity around expectations, create healthy boundaries so your children feel safe, and develop systems to allow consistency to flourish in your home. As a family, you will look back on the times you were at your best, and from those stories, make a list of your family's unique values, which you can return to again and again as guideposts.

THE PLAYBOOK AT A GLANCE

In **Exercise One**, we will start with creating a Family Bedtime Ritual. That's essential because we believe that The Miracle Morning really starts the night before. Next, in **Exercise Two**, we will help you customize a plan to fit your Miracle Morning into your family life for yourself and your kids.

If you only do one exercise in this book, we'd suggest you do **Exercise Three**, Your Unique Family Values. It's not like any values exercise you've done before and will extract the values you've already been living and teaching your kids into a list you can use as teaching tools and guideposts that one day could be passed down through the generations of your family.

After that, in **Exercise Four**, we will walk you step by step through cocreating a S.T.A.R.R. System for your family that will help you manage Screen Time, Allowance, Responsibilities, and Rewards for your children. Next, **Exercise Five** will help you create a Family Screen-Time Contract to get everyone on the same page around electronics use and rules in your household. Everyone will sign it, and it will help you solve so many issues before they even come up. In **Exercise Six**, we will take you through a process to create some goals as a family where you can model this behavior for your kids, and they will learn to do it for themselves, too.

Finally, once you have these systems up and running, you will want to keep meeting regularly as a family. That is where **Exercise Seven** comes into play. You will come up with an agenda for a consistent family meeting (or whatever you decide to call yours). We had a hard time ordering these exercises because they have all come to work together in our household. We put them in the order that made the most sense to us, but I suggest reading through this book and then deciding which order makes the most sense to you and your family. You may want to design your family meeting agenda first to establish that habit before tackling the rest.

After completing this playbook as a family, you will all be on the same page, and you will inevitably need to return to these pages to tweak and update what you've created. As your kids grow, their needs change, and the beauty of these exercises is that you can do them more than once. Some of these exercises we have only done once; others, we've revisited several times until we felt it was just right; others, we do every year, and some we only revisit as needed. We do not have teenagers yet, but we have worked with families with teens, and I strongly believe it's never too late to pass on good habits or family values. Chances are, you've already been teaching them by the way you live your life. Now, it's time to get more purposeful about articulating what's important to your family and creating systems to make sure your kids will leave the house with a strong moral compass.

A construct I live my life by is to have flexibility within structure. A structure that is too firm will typically break under the pressure of everyday life, and one that is too loose will not provide healthy boundaries. This book will help you create some structure in your home, and if something isn't working, change it until it does. The outputs of these exercises are living documents. Nothing is ever permanent unless you say it is. There are no rules except to have fun!

We designed this book to facilitate powerful discussions in your family, but ultimately, whatever you create is yours and is unique to your family. We will share our family stories throughout the book with examples of what we use in our home. Feel free to borrow anything that resonates with you, and please understand that the cocreation piece is crucial. If you don't go through the process with your kids and just take what we created and use it as your own, your kids will not have bought into it, and it will most likely backfire. Worse still is an authoritarian parenting style where the parents create the values or systems and then expect the kids to follow them with no say and to be punished harshly when they don't comply.

HOW TO USE THIS PLAYBOOK

Each exercise in the book is laid out the same way. We'll move through the following questions together:

- Why is it important?
- How did we do it?
- What does the final product look like?

Then, it will be your turn to do the exercise as a family. We will let you know what supplies you will need and the objective of the exercise; then, we will walk you through, step by step. In this playbook, we will provide worksheets to help guide you through each exercise. You can use them to capture your answers to the guiding questions, or you can simply write on blank paper or sticky notes. If you need additional worksheets, you can download blank copies of any of the worksheets on the resource page for this playbook (www.miraclemorning.com/parentsplaybook).

In general, for each exercise, you will need your whole family present. We like to use a freestanding tabletop easel, sticky notes, and markers when we do family exercises. Each family member will get their own worksheet, a pile of sticky notes, and a marker to write or draw their ideas. Sticky notes are nice because you can easily move them around to group similar thoughts together. Markers simply show up a little better than anything else. You're free to do the exercises any way you see fit, but this has been the most effective way for us. You can also use a wall or large whiteboard instead of investing in an easel.

One question we often get from people is: "At what age can we start creating these systems with our kids?" Our kids were about three and seven when we started practicing The Miracle Morning and did our first values exercise. Since then, we've added systems and started having consistent weekly family meetings when the kids were about four and eight. I'm not an expert, but I don't think there is an age that is too young. Obviously, a baby isn't going to be a full participant, but the earlier they get to witness their family members having meaningful conversations about things that matter, the better. In my experience, by age four or five, a child is mature enough to give real input.

Another question we get (usually from people with toddlers or teens) is: "How do we get them to come to the table if they are resistant?" Our answer is an old sales tactic called the Takeaway Close. Leave the choice up to your kids if they want to join you or not, but if they choose not to show up, they won't get a say in important family matters. You, as the parents, will decide everything for them and will fill them in later with any changes to the house rules, family goals, and future adventures. Kids of all ages love to have a say in "the rules," so grant them that courtesy. If they choose not to show up for the exercise, make sure you do fill them in on what the rest of the family decided, and be clear that you expect them to follow whatever was decided in the meeting. Another strategy that works well, especially for tweens and toddlers, is to have snacks available during the meeting. Remember, the more fun you can make the meeting, the more likely you are to get good participation and relevant outcomes.

To get started, we'd suggest reading through the whole book first to decide which exercise you want to do first. We'd also suggest consistently setting aside about an hour or so as a family to go through this playbook one exercise at a time in whatever order you think is best. If your family already has a great system in place for any of the sections, feel free to skip it. The only part you need to read as a family is the **Your Turn** section and the provided worksheet to help guide you through the exercise. The other parts are mainly for your information and to get a sense of what the finished product could look like. Your final product may look vastly different from ours, and that's great. Every family is different, and yours will be different from ours.

As you may have noticed in this section, this book is written from Lindsay's perspective for ease of reading. I, Lindsay, will be your guide, but rest assured, Mike and I are a team and developed these exercises together. Okay, now that we've gotten all that out of the way, let's dive in!

EXERCISE ONE: YOUR FAMILY BEDTIME RITUAL

*"Ironically, to my children, bedtime is a punishment
that violates their basic rights as human beings.
Once the lights are out, you can expect at least an hour
of inmates clanging their tin cups on the cell bars."*

—Jim Gaffigan, comedian

WHY IS IT IMPORTANT?

If you ask long-time Miracle Morning practitioners, most will tell you that a great morning starts the night before. To be excited to wake up in the morning and work on your personal development, you have to be well-rested. If you're going to be waking up earlier than you're used to, you have to also start going to bed earlier than you're used to in order to account for that time. It sounds like a no-brainer, but there are many factors at play here, which makes it surprisingly challenging.

There are so many benefits of getting a great night of sleep, and it literally improves every system of the body. During sleep, our memory is consolidated, our hearts slow down, and our bodies recover and repair themselves. Better sleep improves our mental clarity, focus, and reaction time. It also positively affects growth and stress hormones, the immune system, appetite, breathing, blood pressure, and cardiovascular health. Our sleep is so important that we made this the first exercise in this book.

If you have a baby at home who still wakes in the night, you are probably experiencing firsthand the adverse effects of sleep deprivation. Luckily, it's usually a short-lived stage of development, and the family will all be able to sleep through the night soon. If you suffer from insomnia, sleep apnea, or another issue preventing you from getting the proper amount of shut-eye, please seek professional help to get your sleep back on track. Sleep is so essential for our health; it cannot be put off.

There is a lot of research out there about how much sleep humans need to function at their best. Too much, too little, or too broken up is not ideal. According to the CDC's website, adults need between seven to eight hours of sleep per night. Babies (newborn to age one) should sleep between twelve and sixteen hours a day, including naps. Young children (age two to five) need at least ten hours of sleep, including naps, while school-age children, including teenagers, need at least nine hours of rest each night. That is important information to know when we start the exercise to reverse engineer your bedtime.

Sleep experts recognize the importance of having a consistent bedtime routine for both children and adults. As humans, we are creatures of habit. That can play to our advantage when our rituals are carefully crafted, and it can also play to our disadvantage when we pick up bad habits by default. A consistent, purposefully created bedtime ritual will help our bodies recognize when it's time to wind down and settle into sleep more easily.

Generally, you want to start your bedtime ritual thirty to sixty minutes before you'd like to be asleep. Your bedtime ritual is fully customizable, but here are some good elements to choose from:

- Limit electronics. That glow from your electronics emits a blue light frequency that has been proven to disrupt sleep patterns. It's best to turn them off at least an hour before you'd like to be asleep. If you absolutely must use your computer late at night, you can purchase blue-blocking glasses or screen protectors to help mitigate the adverse effects.

- Dim the lights. Just as the light from electronics can mess with your circadian rhythm, so can bright overhead lights. If your lights don't have dimmer switches, it could be a good investment, or you can get some lamps that don't emit as much light as the overhead lights and use them in the evening.

- Slow down your movement. Exercise is great for your health, but it can actually keep you up if you do it too close to bedtime. Some light stretching or yoga can be a great way to help your body slow down for bedtime, but save your high-intensity workouts for earlier in the day.

- Practice meditation or focused breathing. The benefits of meditation have been known to many since ancient times, and modern science is understanding more and more about them all the time. There are many guided meditation apps to follow, or you can do it free form by simply counting your breath.

- Journal. Anxiety is a big reason people have trouble sleeping. They can't turn off their minds. A great tool to combat that problem is to journal before bed. You can do a brain dump to get all the things that have been floating around in your head down on paper; you can write out a to-do list for the next day, so you can hit the ground running in the morning, journal about your day, or anything else that feels good to you.

- Read. This is often something we incorporate into our kids' bedtimes, and it's also a great way for adults to wind down. It's best to stick to paperbacks or audio versions, so you're not bringing in any unwanted light. Also, you may want to avoid certain exciting genres like suspense or mystery just before bed.

- Take a warm bath or shower. To prepare for sleep, our bodies produce melatonin, and our core body temperature drops. It sounds counterintuitive, but according to the sleep doctor, Michael Breus, taking a warm shower or bath an hour or two before bed makes the body temperature spike, helping your temperature drop more quickly, inducing sleepiness. You can supercharge your bath with a few drops of lavender oil.

- Play soothing music. Music is a great way to calm your mind to drop into rest. But just like reading, choose wisely. Other sounds can also be helpful, like white noise or nature sounds. They can mask unnatural sounds that many find irritating and that keep them awake.

- Prep for the morning. Sometimes, there are just too many things to do in the morning in a limited amount of time. Get some of them out of the way the night before. You can choose your clothes for the next day, pack a healthy lunch, set out a glass of water to rehydrate first thing in the morning, or anything else that will save you time in the morning. Also, lay out anything you will need for your Miracle Morning.

- Self-massage. A massage is certainly a luxury, and it's one you can give to yourself. Spend a little time rubbing your aching feet, shoulders, or hands. That is something you can do for your children to help them settle down for bed, or you and your partner can take turns swapping massages.

- Have a cup of herbal tea or warm milk. Milk contains tryptophan, the same thing turkey has that makes you want to take a nap after Thanksgiving dinner. It's a hormone that induces sleep. A nice glass of warm milk close to bedtime can help you doze off peacefully. As an alternative, herbal teas containing chamomile, valerian root, lemon balm, lavender, passionflower, or magnolia bark have been known to help calm the body. Just make sure to avoid any tea with caffeine.

- Cool down your room or bed. Our body temperature drops about a degree at night. That signals the body it's time to get some shut-eye. To help the process along, turn your thermostat down. You can also buy special sheets that help your bed feel cooler and bed systems that pump cool water through tubes to cool your mattress without using as much energy as your central AC unit.

- Declutter your space. When our physical space is cluttered, it can cause our anxiety to spike, which doesn't help us sleep. I don't suggest taking on your messy closet right before bed, but once your space is organized, it's easy to take a few minutes before bed to put things back in their place, so you're organized for the next day.

- Take care of your personal hygiene. That can range from the basics of bathing, brushing your teeth and hair, all the way to removing your makeup and an extensive skincare regimen. The main thing is to be consistent, so it will trigger your brain that it's time to get ready to sleep.

Everyone knows it's desirable to get a good night's rest, and a simple way to get everyone on the same page with bedtime is to create a simple checklist. That will help create the habit, and before long, you may not need it anymore. As Greg McKeown says in his book *Effortless*, "The beauty of the checklist is that the thinking has been done ahead of time. It's been taken out of the equation, or rather it has been baked into the equation. So, instead of getting these essential things right occasionally, we get them right every time. A cheat sheet is one of the most effective ways, albeit low tech tools we have at our disposal to automate almost anything that really matters." Sometimes the simplest solutions are the best.

HOW DID WE DO IT?

When Ember entered our family, our typical family bedtime routine was for Mike and me to divide and conquer. He would put Tyler to bed, and I would put Ember to bed. Tyler was four when Ember was born, so he was pretty independent with bedtime already. He would get his pajamas on, brush and floss his teeth, and brush his hair. Then Mike would read him a bedtime story, and Tyler would drift off to sleep afterward.

Ember's bedtime ritual was also pretty simple. As a baby, she was easy. I would feed her, rock and swaddle her, and gently lay her down. She slept six hours at night from day one: a dream come true! Once the kids were in bed, Mike and I had time to do our own bedtime rituals.

However, as Ember entered toddlerhood, she literally demanded to be read a bedtime story like her brother. She also would not fall asleep if I left the room. She would cry or get out of bed repeatedly until I gave up and came to lie with her until she was asleep. It often meant I'd fall asleep in her room and wake up in the middle of the night to head to my bed. That was not working for Mike or me, and something had to give.

We all have a current bedtime ritual, whether we recognize it as such or not. Ember's bedtime routine was sucking the life out of us, and I was not getting the quality of sleep I needed or the time with Mike I had enjoyed previously. The first step to making positive change is awareness. We decided to redesign our bedtime ritual as a family with this simple exercise.

1. Review your current bedtime ritual.
2. Ask, "What do we need to *keep* doing (or do more of)?"
3. Ask, "What do we need to *start* doing?"
4. Ask, "What do we need to *stop* doing?" Turn them into positive actions.
5. Reverse engineer your ideal bedtime.
6. Put it all together into your Family Bedtime Ritual Checklist.

STEP ONE: REVIEW YOUR CURRENT BEDTIME RITUAL.

- Our current bedtime routine was very disjointed. I didn't get to spend any time with Tyler or Mike at bedtime. Ember monopolized my time, which made it difficult for me to get enough sleep.

STEP TWO: ASK, "WHAT DO WE NEED TO KEEP DOING (OR DO MORE OF)?"

- Read a bedtime story. Both Tyler and Ember enjoyed having stories read to them at night, so that was an element we wanted to keep that worked for everyone.
- Take care of personal hygiene. Bath time was also something both kids enjoyed, and good personal hygiene habits are important to build from an early age.
- Use a sound machine. Both kids liked to have noise in the background to fall asleep to, so that was something we would keep as part of their bedtime rituals.

STEP THREE: ASK, "WHAT DO WE NEED TO START DOING?"

- Help Ember fall asleep by herself. I told Ember that staying in her room each night meant I wasn't getting to do the things I need to do before *my* bedtime, and it was making me grumpy. Even as a toddler, she was able to grasp that it was a problem. I asked her if there was a reason she didn't like to go to sleep by herself and if we could come up with a solution together. We discovered she was afraid to go to sleep because she thought a bear was going to eat her up. I have no idea where she got that idea. At the time, we lived in a suburb of Philadelphia, and bears are not native to that area. Obviously, it was not a legitimate fear, but toddlers do not yet have a fully functioning prefrontal cortex and don't really *do logic,* so there's no reason to argue. If she had the idea in her head that it was true, then for all intents and purposes, it was true. I was not going to argue with her reality. Instead, I decided to get creative. A friend of mine had recently given us some essential oil spray that included lavender. I told Ember it was "bear spray" and asked if she would feel safe if I made sure to spray it each night? She agreed she would, so we added that to the list.
- Use "bear spray." Mom will spray the lavender spray each night to keep bears away.
- Add a night light. Ember also said her room was too dark at night, so we agreed to add a night light to her room. We knew a nightlight could also counteract healthy sleep habits if it was too bright or emitted blue light, so we were choosy about our night light.
- Read all together. Both our kids loved bedtime stories, and I liked the idea of all of us hearing the same book, so we decided we would read aloud as a family at bedtime.

STEP FOUR: ASK, "WHAT DO WE NEED TO *STOP* DOING?" TURN THEM INTO POSITIVE ACTIONS.

- Stop getting out of bed. Ember would often get out of bed for a glass of water or to tell us she was scared or for some other reason to delay bedtime. We could counteract that with a little preparation. We started putting a water bottle next to her bed so she could fill it herself in the bathroom, and we agreed to add the night light and "bear spray" to cut down on her fears. The positive action is, "Stay in bed until morning."

- Stop using screen time within one hour of bedtime. Like many parents, we're tired at the end of the day. It's easy to just turn the TV on or hand your child an iPad to decompress after a long day. However, that can mess with their sleep cycle, so it often backfires, and kids have more trouble falling asleep. After we learned that, we made a commitment to have "electronic bedtime" at 8 p.m. Try setting a sleep timer, so the TV automatically goes off at the designated time. The positive action is, "Put electronics to bed at 8 p.m."

- Stop drinking milk after brushing teeth. Our kids also had a bad habit of drinking milk right before bedtime. While drinking warm milk can be part of a healthy bedtime ritual since it contains the sleep hormone tryptophan, it's not a good idea to drink it *after* you brush your teeth since milk also contains naturally occurring sugar, called lactose. Drinking right before bed can also make overnight accidents more common, so we decided to move beverages thirty minutes before bedtime. We set our Amazon Echo (Alexa) to make an announcement at 7:30 p.m. each night for "last call." That way, no one had to spend any mental energy on it. The announcement also serves as a reminder to set a sleep timer on any electronics in use to automatically turn off at 8:00. For more helpful hints to use Alexa in your parenting, check out my blog post, *How Alexa Can be Your Parenting Ally*, at www.GratefulParent.com. The positive action is, "Last call for milk is 7:30 p.m."

- What you produce at the end of this exercise should be as concise as possible and only include the things you *are* going to do. Turn your "Stop Doing" items into the things you *will* do instead. Our brains only respond to things in the positive. For example, if I told you, "Don't think about a white bear," you would have just thought about a white bear. Putting the words *stop*, *don't*, or *no* in front of something isn't effective. For example, instead of saying, "Don't get out of bed," say, "Stay in bed until morning."

STEP FIVE: REVERSE ENGINEER IDEAL BEDTIME.

- Our kids were three and eight when we did this exercise. According to the CDC, they needed at least nine to ten hours of sleep. They generally woke up around 7:00 a.m. on their own, so if we count back ten hours, they should be asleep by 9:00 p.m. each night. That meant we had to start their bedtime ritual at 8:00 p.m.

STEP SIX: PUT IT ALL TOGETHER INTO YOUR FAMILY BEDTIME RITUAL CHECKLIST.

- You've done all the thinking; now it's time to put it into a checklist for the kids to follow each night.

WHAT DOES THE FINISHED PRODUCT LOOK LIKE?

Here is an example of a checklist for bedtime. We no longer use this checklist because all of these things have become habits, and we don't need it anymore; but checklists are a great way to build new habits.

7:30 p.m.

☐ Last call for milk (Alexa reminder)

8:00 p.m.

☐ Electronics Bedtime: Please put them to bed outside your bedroom.

☐ Shower or wash face.

☐ Put pajamas on.

☐ Brush teeth.

☐ Floss teeth.

☐ Brush hair.

☐ Fill up water bottle.

☐ Set out clothes for tomorrow.

☐ Read aloud.

☐ Use "bear spray."

☐ Listen to sound machine or audiobook on 30-minute sleep timer.

9:00 p.m.

☐ Turn lights out.

☐ Stay in bedroom until 7:00 a.m.

—YOUR TURN—
CREATE YOUR FAMILY BEDTIME RITUAL

SUPPLIES:

- Your family
- This Playbook
- Your Family Miracle Morning Worksheet or a blank piece of paper (you can download additional copies of the worksheets from www.miraclemorning.com/parentsplaybook)
- Pen or pencil

OBJECTIVE:

The goal of this activity is to create a family bedtime checklist.

This exercise has six steps:

1. Review your current bedtime ritual

2. Ask: "What do we need to keep doing (or do more of)?"

3. Ask: "What do we need to start doing?"

4. Ask: "What do we need to stop doing?" Turn them into positive actions.

5. Reverse engineer the ideal bedtime.

6. Put it all together into your Family Bedtime Ritual Checklist.

STEP ONE: REVIEW YOUR CURRENT BEDTIME RITUAL.

Think about your family's current bedtime ritual. Every family has a ritual, whether the members recognize it or not. The first step to making a positive change is awareness. Write out your current routine here:

_____

_____

_____

_____

_____

_____

_____

STEP TWO: WHAT DO WE NEED TO KEEP DOING (OR DO MORE OF)?

Any elements of bedtime that have been working for everyone in the family should be kept. If there is something that works for one member but not everyone, try to think of a solution that would be a win-win for all involved.

_____

_____

_____

_____

_____

_____

STEP THREE: "WHAT DO WE NEED TO START DOING?"

Think about some of the elements of a healthy bedtime ritual listed earlier and consider adding one of them to your new family bedtime ritual.

_____

_____

_____

_____

_____

_____

STEP FOUR: WHAT DO WE NEED TO STOP DOING? AND TURN THEM INTO A POSITIVE ACTION.

Sometimes bad habits form when we aren't intentional about creating them. That's okay, and we can change them now. Anything you've identified as a bad habit goes here. Anything you identify here, you'll want to turn it around to make it something you want to start doing. For example, if you said you want to "Stop watching TV before bed," you will want to turn it into a positive action. Investigate why you're not turning the TV off. Is it that your settings are set to automatically play the next episode? Is it because you can't find the remote? Is it because you don't know how to set the sleep timer? Once you know the reason, you can add that to your checklist. "Set a 30-minute sleep timer for TV at 7:30 p.m."

_____

_____

_____

_____

_____

STEP FIVE: REVERSE ENGINEER AN IDEAL BEDTIME.

Time to do some simple math. Whatever time you need to be up, count backward to make sure you're getting enough sleep based on the recommendations earlier in this chapter. For example, if your kids need to be up by 7:00 a.m. to get ready for school and out the door and they need ten hours of sleep, they should be asleep by 9:00 p.m., which means their bedtime ritual should start around 8:00 p.m. If you want to wake at 6:00 a.m. to have an hour for your Miracle Morning and need eight hours of sleep, your bedtime is 10:00 p.m., so your bedtime ritual should start at 9:00 p.m.

STEP SIX: PUT IT ALL TOGETHER INTO YOUR FAMILY BEDTIME RITUAL CHECKLIST.

Use this space to write out your Family Bedtime Ritual Checklist.

Time for Last Call: _____

Electronics Bedtime: _____

Kids Asleep by: _____

BEDTIME CHECKLIST

- _____
- _____
- _____
- _____
- _____
- _____
- _____
- _____

OTHER IMPORTANT STEPS OR BEDTIME RULES FOR YOUR FAMILY:

- _____
- _____
- _____
- _____
- _____
- _____
- _____

EXERCISE TWO:
YOUR FAMILY MIRACLE MORNING

"It is well to be up before daybreak,
for such habits contribute to health, wealth, and wisdom."

—Jim Gaffigan, comedian

WHY IS IT IMPORTANT?

If you have not read a Miracle Morning book, I highly recommend you pick up a copy of the original or one of the others in the series. The series books all summarize the original and offer some extras for their target audience. Mike and I are the co-authors on *The Miracle Morning for Parents and Families*, so we're partial to that one, but there is also a version for College Students, Couples, Salespeople, Real Estate Agents, Writers, Entrepreneurs, Millionaires, Teachers, Network Marketers, Addiction Recovery, and the *Art of Affirmations* coloring book. Many of the books are translated into several different languages. In 2020, Hal also released *The Miracle Morning* movie, which is a great way to learn about it during a family movie night!

It has been said, "If you win the morning, you win the day." I believe that to be true, and I love the framework Hal has created with his Life S.A.V.E.R.S. It's an acronym that stands for Silence, Affirmations, Visualization, Exercise, Reading, and Scribing. When Hal created his Miracle Morning, he was in a low place and researched what the most successful people do to start their days. That's how he compiled the S.A.V.E.R.S. Many people do one or two of those things, and he was curious what would happen if he did all six. Spoiler Alert: He discovered success and happiness.

When I committed to The Miracle Morning, I was pumped. I set my alarm clock early, I got up and did my Life S.A.V.E.R.S., and I felt unstoppable—until a week later when our youngest, she was three at the time, started coming in and interrupting me. My first response was to sit her in front of the TV so that I could finish my Miracle Morning. Huge mistake! Yes, I could finish in peace, but afterward, all hell broke loose as I tried to get her away from the TV and ready for the day ahead. My next idea was to let her play quietly in the room with me as I did my practice. That worked much better, and to my surprise, she came to me one morning and said, "Mommy, I want to do what you're doing."

It had never dawned on me to teach my kids to do their own Miracle Morning ritual, and I couldn't believe it took the wisdom of my three-year-old to give me that idea. A lot of people turn to personal development when they hit a rough spot in their lives, but to kids, it looks like play. If we can teach our kids how to start their day from an early age, they will be way ahead of the game as they reach adulthood. As happy-go-lucky kids, Tyler and Ember had a hard time connecting with the acronym S.A.V.E.R.S. As a family, we created a new acronym for kids called C.H.A.R.M.S.: Creativity, Health, Affirmations, Reading, Meditation, and Service. It's mostly the same practices but more kid-friendly and with the additional practice of service, which is one of our family values.

HOW DID WE DO IT?

We had a loose framework for each of us to have our own Miracle Morning, but we needed to get more specific and create a *plan* to put it into action. First, we committed to doing a 30-day challenge as a family. That way, we could hold each other accountable and support each other when the going got tough. We got out some paper and started brainstorming ideas for each of the S.A.V.E.R.S. and C.H.A.R.M.S. Once we had a good menu of options for each element of The Miracle Morning, we made a plan for the week. We thought about what time we would wake up, where we would each do our Miracle Morning, what we would do during the week for each of the elements, and how many minutes we would do each one. We wrote out our plan on a piece of paper, creating a simple tracker. Then, we were ready to get started!

Inevitably, your routine will become stale, or you will fall off the wagon. It happens to the best of us. The trick is not to beat yourself up about it and simply revisit your menu of options, revise your plan, and recommit. Kids tend to get bored a little more quickly than adults. They may need to return to their menu of ideas more often to switch things up. You may want to encourage them to come up with lots and lots of ideas and maybe even ways to combine C.H.A.R.M.S. to knock out two birds with one stone. For example, they could write a nice note to someone for creativity and service. Or they could do jumping jacks while saying their affirmations to complete health and affirmations. A helpful strategy I learned from James Clear in his book *Atomic Habits* is called "habit stacking." It's when you attach a new habit to an already established habit. For example, you may already drink a cup of coffee each morning. You could start stacking the habit of affirmations onto that existing habit. Every time you start the coffee maker, you recite your affirmations while it's brewing.

If you're curious, we do not wake our kids up early to do their Miracle Morning. We also don't force them to do it. They have the option to do it once they're awake. If your children are older, they can choose to wake up early on their own to complete their Miracle Morning, but I would not encourage you to obligate them to it. Our kids have always had the choice to do their C.H.A.R.M.S. or not, but as part of our family screen-time contract (we'll get to that in another exercise), they are not allowed any screen time until all six are completed. Some days, it takes them all day to complete their Miracle Morning, and some days, they don't do it at all. We want to give them the leeway to make mistakes and experiment to see how they feel on the days they do their Miracle Morning and when they don't. It's all a learning experience.

WHAT DOES THE FINISHED PRODUCT LOOK LIKE?

PARENT WORKSHEET

STEP ONE: MAKE A COMMITMENT TO COMPLETE A 30-DAY MIRACLE MORNING CHALLENGE.

I, <u>Lindsay McCarthy</u>, commit to completing the Miracle Morning every day for the next thirty days. I will begin my 30-Day Challenge on November 1st, 2021, and my 30-Day Challenge will be completed on November 30th, 2021.

Signed: <u>*Lindsay McCarthy*</u>

Date: <u>October 31st, 2021</u>

STEP TWO: CREATE A MENU OF OPTIONS AND LIST YOUR FAVORITE IDEAS FOR HOW YOU WILL COMPLETE EACH ELEMENT OF THE MIRACLE MORNING.

SILENCE IDEAS

- Insight Timer App—try different lengths and voices
- Drink tea in silence outside while listening to the birds
- Do a mindful breathing exercise.

AFFIRMATION IDEAS

- Include favorite quote: "Our deepest fear is not that we are inadequate. Our deepest fear is that we are powerful beyond measure. It is our light, not our darkness that most frightens us. We ask ourselves, 'Who am I to be brilliant, gorgeous, talented, fabulous?' Actually, who are you not to be? You are a child of God. Your playing small does not serve the world. There is nothing enlightened about shrinking so that other people won't feel insecure around you. We are all meant to shine, as children do. We were born to make manifest the glory of God that is within us. It's not just in some of us; it's in everyone. And as we let our own light shine, we unconsciously give other people permission to do the same. As we are liberated from our own fear, our presence automatically liberates others." —Marianne Williamson

- Include Brené Brown's 10 Guideposts for Wholehearted Living.
- Include my top priority goal.

VISUALIZATION IDEAS

- Create a vision board.
- Walk myself through the day.
- Visualize achieving my top goal.

EXERCISE IDEAS

- Create an ideal schedule for the week with variety.
- Run 2x week.
- Do yoga 1x week.
- Lift weights 2x week.

READING IDEAS

- Do a daily devotional.
- Listen to audiobook in the car.
- Read personal development books.

SCRIBING IDEAS

- Search journal prompts for the month and print out.
- Use the 5-minute journal app.
- Write down three takeaways from my reading today.

S.A.V.E.R.S. HABIT STACKING IDEAS

- Listen to an audiobook while I exercise.
- Say affirmations after I brush my teeth in the morning.
- Listen to a guided meditation while I brew my tea.
- Have a dance party with the kids while I make breakfast.
- Read and journal while the kids eat breakfast.

OTHER THINGS

- Eat breakfast.
- Pack kids' lunches.
- Do the family hug.

STEP THREE: WRITE OUT A PLAN FOR YOUR FIRST MIRACLE MORNING.

Where will you complete your Miracle Morning? In the kitchen

Start Time: 6:30 a.m.

- Silence Activity and # of Minutes: Insight timer guided meditation for 10 Minutes
- Affirmation Activity and # of Minutes: Read my affirmations while my tea kettle is heating up
- Visualization Activity and # of Minutes: Study my vision board for 1 minute
- Exercise Activity and # of Minutes: 7 Minute App for 7 minutes
- Reading Activity and # of Minutes: Read Science of Mind Daily Reading for 10 minutes
- Scribing Activity and # of Minutes: Journal for 5 minutes

End Time: 7:04 a.m.

Other Things I will do to be ready for my day: Eat a healthy breakfast, pack kids' lunches, family hug.

KID WORKSHEET

STEP ONE: MAKE A COMMITMENT TO COMPLETE A 30-DAY MIRACLE MORNING CHALLENGE.

I, <u>Tyler McCarthy</u>, commit to completing The Miracle Morning every day for the next thirty days. I will begin my 30-Day Challenge on <u>November 1st, 2021</u>, and my 30-Day Challenge will be completed on <u>November 30th, 2021</u>.

Signed: *Tyler McCarthy*

Date: <u>October 31st, 2021</u>

STEP TWO: CREATE A MENU OF OPTIONS AND LIST YOUR FAVORITE IDEAS FOR HOW YOU WILL COMPLETE EACH ELEMENT OF THE MIRACLE MORNING.

CREATIVITY IDEAS

- Color in *The Miracle Morning Art of Affirmations* coloring book.
- Build a house with Legos.
- Make a pretend meal with Play-Doh.
- Paint.
- Draw.
- Write in my journal.
- Create affirmations book.
- Make a list of books I'd like to read this year or subjects I'm interested in.

HEALTH IDEAS

- Eat a healthy breakfast.
- Brush my teeth and hair.
- Have a dance party in the kitchen with my family.
- Do the 7-minute app exercises.
- Do jumping jacks at the bus stop.

AFFIRMATION IDEAS

- Create affirmations that follow the alphabet.
- Find printable affirmation cards online to recite.
- Make an affirmations jar.

READING IDEAS

- Ask a sibling or parent to read to me.
- Listen to an audiobook during breakfast or while I'm getting dressed.
- Practice reading with a book I can read myself.

MEDITATION IDEAS

- Search for kids' meditations on YouTube.
- Sit in silence for 3 minutes—set a timer.
- Do a walking meditation on the way to the bus stop.

SERVICE IDEAS

- Feed the dog.
- Make tea or coffee for Mom.
- Pack a sibling's lunch.
- Leave flowers for a neighbor on my way to the bus stop.
- Leave a nice note for my mom or dad to find.
- Help my sibling to clean their room.
- Water the plants.

C.H.A.R.M.S. COMBINATIONS

- Read to my sibling (Reading and Service).
- Take the dog for a run (Health and Service).
- Say my affirmations while doing squats (Affirmations and Health).
- Lead a guided meditation for the whole family (Meditation and Service).
- Write a nice note to someone (Creativity and Service).
- Create an obstacle course to do for exercise (Creativity and Health).
- Listen to an audiobook while I walk to the bus stop (Reading and Health).

OTHER THINGS I HAVE TO DO BEFORE I'M READY FOR MY DAY

- Get dressed.
- Eat breakfast.
- Pack my backpack.

STEP THREE: WRITE OUT A PLAN FOR YOUR FIRST MIRACLE MORNING.

Where will you complete your Miracle Morning:? <u>Kitchen</u>

Start Time: <u>7:30 a.m.</u>

- Creativity Activity and # of Minutes: <u>Build a house with Legos for 5 minutes.</u>
- Health Activity and # of Minutes: <u>Eat a healthy breakfast and have a family dance party for 10 minutes.</u>
- Affirmations Activity and # of Minutes: <u>Say my ABC affirmations out loud for 1 minute.</u>
- Reading Activity and # of Minutes: <u>Practice reading for 5 minutes.</u>
- Meditation Activity and # of Minutes: <u>Sit in silence with a timer for 3 minutes.</u>
- Service Activity and # of Minutes: <u>Make a cup of tea for Mom for 5 minutes.</u>

End Time: <u>7:59 am</u>

Other Things I will do to be ready for my day: Get dressed and pack my backpack.

–YOUR TURN–
CUSTOMIZE YOUR FAMILY MIRACLE MORNING

SUPPLIES:

- Your family
- This Playbook
- Your Family Miracle Morning Worksheet or a blank piece of paper (you can download additional copies of the worksheets from www.miraclemorning.com/parentsplaybook)
- Pen or pencil

OBJECTIVE:

By the end of this exercise, each family member will have a fully customized Miracle Morning ritual.

THIS EXERCISE HAS FIVE STEPS:

1. Make a commitment to complete a 30-Day Miracle Morning Challenge.
2. Create a Menu of Options for each of the S.A.V.E.R.S. or C.H.A.R.M.S.
3. Write out a plan for your first Miracle Morning.
4. Follow your plan.
5. Revisit, revise, and recommit.

STEP ONE: MAKE A COMMITMENT TO COMPLETE A 30-DAY MIRACLE MORNING CHALLENGE.

If you're brand-new to The Miracle Morning, our suggestion is to schedule a family movie night to watch *The Miracle Morning* movie (https://miraclemorning.com/movie/) or read or listen to one of The Miracle Morning series books as a family. That will get your family fired up to want to commit to a 30-Day Miracle Morning Challenge. For the next month, commit to waking up thirty to sixty minutes earlier than you normally do and spend your morning doing the S.A.V.E.R.S. or C.H.A.R.M.S. On the worksheet under Step One, there is a place for you to sign your name to the 30-Day challenge; that will help underscore your commitment to completing the challenge.

When we wrote *The Miracle Morning for Parents and Families*, one of the bonuses that came with the book was a C.H.A.R.M.S. Tracker. Having a tracker is a great way to build a habit. Our kids have been doing C.H.A.R.M.S. for years, and they still track it as part of their daily S.T.A.R.R. Chart (more on that later). If you would like to download a copy and find other resources to help you get started on your 30-Day Miracle Morning challenge, check out https://miraclemorning.com/bonuses-downloads-resources-parents/

STEP TWO: CREATE A MENU OF OPTIONS FOR EACH OF THE S.A.V.E.R.S. OR C.H.A.R.M.S.

When you first get started, you will need to decide how you will approach each element of the C.H.A.R.M.S. or S.A.V.E.R.S. There are many suggestions contained within the Miracle Morning books and movie. The possibilities are endless, and empowering each person to choose their practice for each element will help make it more fun and meaningful, leading to better outcomes. During this 30-Day Challenge, experiment with as many variations of each element as you can. That will help you create a plan that works for you to successfully continue The Miracle Morning. Also, experiment with the order in which you do them.

You can try a strategy called "habit stacking," or combine some of the S.A.V.E.R.S. or C.H.A.R.M.S. to save time in the morning. We all have things we do each morning, like eating breakfast or brushing our teeth. Try adding one of the S.A.V.E.R.S. or C.H.A.R.M.S. to an existing habit. For example, to make reading in the morning a habit, you could start listening to an audiobook while you're eating breakfast. That way, you're not adding time to your morning, but you are still adding a positive habit.

Set a timer for ten minutes, and using the worksheets, write down as many ideas as you can come up with for each of the S.A.V.E.R.S. (if you're a parent) or C.H.A.R.M.S. (if you're a kid). Also, write down anything else that you have to do before you walk out the door in the morning.

STEP THREE: WRITE OUT YOUR PLAN FOR YOUR FIRST MIRACLE MORNING.

Choose from your menu of options to create a plan for your first week of Miracle Mornings. Remember, you might plan to wake up earlier to fit these activities in. You will set a start and end time for your Miracle Morning and select a good physical space where you will complete the exercises each morning.

STEP FOUR: FOLLOW YOUR PLAN.

You've done the hard part of coming up with a plan; now, all you have to do is follow it!

STEP FIVE: REVISIT, REVISE, AND RECOMMIT.

The Miracle Morning is one of those things that is simple but not easy. Kids get bored easily, and many like a lot of variety. After at least a week, see how your plan has been working out. Do you like the order in which you're doing the elements? If not, experiment with a different order. Are you bored with your exercise routine? Switch it up. Are you still having trouble getting out of bed? Maybe you need an accountability partner or coach (outside of your family). Remember, if you fall off the wagon, don't beat yourself up. Just pick yourself up, dust yourself off, and recommit.

YOUR FAMILY MIRACLE MORNING PARENT WORKSHEET

STEP 1: MAKE A COMMITMENT TO COMPLETE A 30-DAY MIRACLE MORNING CHALLENGE.

I, _____, commit to completing The Miracle Morning every day for the next thirty days. I will begin my 30-Day Challenge on _____ and my 30-Day Challenge will be completed on _____.

Signed: _____

Date:_____

STEP 2: CREATE A MENU OF OPTIONS AND LIST YOUR FAVORITE IDEAS FOR HOW YOU WILL COMPLETE EACH ELEMENT OF THE MIRACLE MORNING BELOW:

SILENCE IDEAS

_____

_____

_____

AFFIRMATION IDEAS

_____

_____

_____

VISUALIZATION IDEAS

_____

_____

_____

EXERCISE IDEAS

_____

_____

_____

READING IDEAS

_____

_____

_____

SCRIBING IDEAS

_____

_____

_____

OTHER THINGS (I HAVE TO DO TO BE READY FOR MY DAY)

_____

_____

_____

STEP 3: WRITE OUT A PLAN FOR YOUR FIRST MIRACLE MORNING.

Where will you complete your Miracle
Morning: _____

Start Time: _____

• Silence Activity and # of Minutes: _____

• Affirmations Activity and # of Minutes: _____

• Visualization Activity and # of Minutes: _____

• Exercise Activity and # of Minutes: _____

• Reading Activity and # of Minutes: _____

• Scribing Activity and # of Minutes: _____

End Time: _____

OTHER THINGS (I HAVE TO DO TO BE READY FOR MY DAY)

_____

_____

_____

YOUR FAMILY MIRACLE MORNING KID'S WORKSHEET

STEP 1: MAKE A COMMITMENT TO COMPLETE A 30-DAY MIRACLE MORNING CHALLENGE.

I, _____, commit to completing The Miracle Morning every day for the next thirty days. I will begin my 30-Day Challenge on _____ and my 30-Day Challenge will be completed on _____.

Signed: _____

Date:_____

STEP 2: CREATE A MENU OF OPTIONS AND LIST YOUR FAVORITE IDEAS FOR HOW YOU WILL COMPLETE EACH ELEMENT OF THE MIRACLE MORNING BELOW:

CREATIVITY IDEAS

_____

_____

_____

HEALTH IDEAS

_____

_____

_____

AFFIRMATION IDEAS

_____

_____

_____

READING IDEAS

_____

_____

_____

MEDITATION IDEAS

_____

_____

_____

SERVICE IDEAS

_____

_____

_____

C.H.A.R.M.S. COMBINATIONS

_____

_____

_____

OTHER THINGS I HAVE TO DO BEFORE I'M READY FOR MY DAY

_____

_____

_____

STEP 3: WRITE OUT A PLAN FOR YOUR FIRST MIRACLE MORNING.

Where will you complete your Miracle
Morning: _____

Start Time: _____

• Creativity Activity and # of Minutes: _____

• Health Activity and # of Minutes: _____

• Affirmations Activity and # of Minutes: _____

• Reading Activity and # of Minutes: _____

• Meditation Activity and # of Minutes: _____

• Service Activity and # of Minutes: _____

End Time: _____

OTHER THINGS I WILL DO TO BE READY FOR MY DAY

_____

_____

_____

EXERCISE THREE: YOUR UNIQUE FAMILY VALUES

*"I come from a large family,
but I was not raised with a fortune.
Something more was left me,
and that was family values."*

—Dikembe Mutombo, professional basketball player

WHY IS IT IMPORTANT?

Mike and I feel blessed to have careers with Keller Williams Realty. The company has clearly defined its mission, vision, values, perspectives, and beliefs. If you walk into a Keller Williams office, you will literally see them written on the walls. Everyone that works for the company is taught these principles and strives to live by them. The expectations for what it means to be a Keller Williams agent are crystal clear. From that model of corporate culture, we wanted to create our unique McCarthy family culture—informed by our values. We wanted our kids to not only know what our values are but live by them and be able to articulate to others what it means to be a McCarthy.

Something Mike likes to say is, "Our legacy is only as strong as the hands we equip to carry it forward." When he says legacy, he is not just talking about a financial legacy (although we hope to create that too). He is talking about creating a family culture that will last for generations to come. It's about sharing family stories and creating rituals and traditions that will be passed down. In a rare interview, David Rockefeller Jr., chairman of Rockefeller & Co. and one of the most well-known and longest-lasting family legacies, said that the family developed a system of values, traditions, and institutions that have helped the family stay together and preserve their wealth. We want to do the same.

We all have a moral compass that guides us. It's a set of beliefs that we pick up by simply being alive and observing others, or we can craft it. We call that set of beliefs our values. We all have values that are present in our families, but some families purposefully define them and use them as a tool to teach their children how to show up in the world, and others don't. In this exercise, we will teach you how to codesign a set of values using your family's stories.

Stories have been used for millennia to pass on principles and lessons from our ancestors. In his book, *Effortless*, Greg McKeown writes, "We love stories. We understand stories. We remember stories, and that means it's easier to share or to teach stories. Stories have the power to turn any audience into a room full of teachers." Using the stories of your ancestors and your current family unit, we will use the Xchange Method and the power of Appreciative Inquiry to define your family's unique values. These are not meant to be aspirational beliefs but the actual values you already live by as a family. All we are doing here is defining them on purpose.

Instead of focusing on improving weaknesses, appreciative inquiry is a tool that uses positive questions to draw out the strengths and unique capabilities of a system—in this case, your family—to build from good to excellent. Another thing we love about Appreciative Inquiry is that all stakeholders have a voice, so it's important to have the entire family involved in creating your family values because more voices and perspectives included will yield better results.

Our values then become a teaching tool to guide our decisions. Our values are transmitted from generation to generation. The power of defining them and sharing them with our children will make the world a better place. Well-defined values give our kids a guidance system to follow. They know how to show up in the world. If you do no other exercise in this book, do this one!

A real-life example of how this works involves our son, Tyler. He was at school one day when I got a call from his teacher that he had cut himself while using a saw. He went to a very progressive school that allowed children to use real tools. They were using saws to cut down invasive species in the nearby forest when Tyler's saw slipped, and he cut his finger.

I had to take him to get stitches. At the hospital, we had to wait a long time for help, and he was so patient. As he was getting some numbing shots in his finger, he closed his eyes and started taking deep breaths.

As the nurse started giving him the stitches, she commented on how brave he was being.

He just looked her in the eyes and said matter-of-factly, "It's because I'm a resilient warrior."

We had given him the words to use to describe the way he was showing up. I was so proud of him for not only living our values but also being able to articulate them to the nurse.

HOW DID WE DO IT?

STEP ONE: REMEMBER STORIES OF WHEN YOU WERE AT YOUR BEST AS A FAMILY

We set aside time on a weekend, and we got out our easel, sticky notes, markers, and journals. We asked the kids to think about times our family was at our best and some of our high-point moments as a family. We told them to think about what strengths our family brought to each of these situations.

Mike and I thought about some stories our parents told us growing up that we wanted to share with the kids to bring previous generations of the family into the exercise.

We set a timer and took ten minutes to journal or draw out our answers.

STEP TWO: SHARE STORIES

Now that we all had our stories in mind, we got in a semicircle, and everyone got some sticky notes and a marker. We went around, starting with the youngest, and each shared one story until everyone shared all their stories. As each person shared, we jotted down different words of themes we pulled out from their story on sticky notes.

STORY EXAMPLES:

Ember: I think our family was at our best when we were skiing together because we love to be outside in nature and active. I loved the fun skiing Easter egg hunt at A-Basin Ski Resort. Mom did the research to find out about it, Dad reserved a parking spot so we could be close to the action, and Mom and Dad came with us on the mountain to collect the eggs. Mom went with me, and Dad went with Tyler since we were in different age groups. Even though we weren't all together the whole time, we had a lot of fun, and we worked as a team.

Easter Egg Hunt Story strengths we brought: athleticism, persistence, teamwork, and love of the outdoors.

Tyler: I think we were at our best when we decided to move to Austin. We made the decision as a family and did a lot of research, and found the best neighborhood and school for our family's lifestyle. Now we are surrounded by some of our best friends in the world, can be outside most of the year, and love the flexibility and structure of our school.

Austin Story strengths we brought: ability to build strong community, purposeful decision, curiosity, and ability to step outside our comfort zone.

Mom: I think we were at our best on our trip to Mexico because we were all fully present on that vacation, and there was something that each of us loved to do at the resort. Tyler and Dad could skateboard. Mom and Ember could play at the beach. There was a kids club for Ember to connect with kids her age and a babysitting service so Mom and Dad could enjoy the nightlife, and there were fun excursions so we could learn about the local area and have fun adventures as a family ziplining.

Mexico Story strengths we brought: an open mind, adventure, support for each other, so everyone gets to do something they want to do, inclusivity, learning, and being present to fully enjoy the vacation.

Dad: My dad told me a story about my Grandpa Rich. He told me that a long time ago, Grandpa Rich stopped to help a man change his flat tire in the rain. Grandpa Rich worked in a factory at the time and didn't have a lot of money. The man he helped was very grateful and offered to give my grandpa a better job. After a year of working for him, the man then trained him to sell insurance where he could earn even more money for his family. My dad, your Grandpa Rich, saw his dad rise through the ranks and made a decision that he, too, could find opportunity and provide even better for his family.

Grandpa Rich Story strengths we brought: integrity, hard work, kindness, leadership, transformation, legacy, and service.

Tyler: I think our family was at our best when we had our yard sale and a goodbye party before we moved to Texas. We all worked together to sell or give away the stuff we didn't want to take to Texas. It was a fun way to say goodbye to all our family and friends in Pennsylvania, and we got rid of a lot of stuff! Win-win. We were generous with the stuff we gave away, and it feels good that a lot of our stuff went to our friends who can make good use of it.

Yard Sale Story strengths we brought: generosity, abundance mindset, teamwork, strong community, leadership, creating win-win situations, and ability to let things go.

Mom: I think we were at our best during the quarantine of 2020. We had a good attitude, and we had a lot of time together to play and learn new things. It gave us time to slow down and not be so busy, which helped us reevaluate what is truly important in life. We also got creative to pass our newly found time.

Quarantine Story strengths we brought: playfulness, faith, resilience, creativity, finding the magic in the mundane, ability to embrace change, learning, and strong community.

Dad: On my mom's side of the family, my Grandpa Joe bought a huge house that was in foreclosure from a bank in Ohio. They had so much space in that house, most of the family moved in, and they used to let people stay there for free. My Grandma Lee would cook meals for everyone and make them feel welcome. It didn't matter if she knew them or not. All were welcome to stay and eat. I even have an old *People* magazine with them on the cover and an article in the magazine about them taking people in and having multiple generations living under the same roof!

Mansion Story strengths we brought: generosity, being kind to all, serving others, bringing people together, and setting a good example.

Dad: I also did a little research on the history of the McCarthy family and found out McCarthy means loving. Our family crest has a stag on it and says, "Fortis ferox et celer," which means "strong, courageous, and swift." And I also looked up our official family motto, "Forti et tibeli nihil difficile," which translates to, "Nothing is difficult to the brave and faithful."

McCarthy Name Story strengths we brought: strength, courage, resilience, warriors, love, bravery, faith, history, and legacy.

STEP THREE: SYNTHESIZE THEMES

By that time, we had sticky notes all over our easel. Then, our job was to look for commonality and group similar themes together. It was easy to move the sticky notes around to group ideas together.

For example, in our stories, some similar words were *serving others* and *service*. Those were grouped together. Generosity was duplicated, so that was grouped together. Leadership, community, and ability to build strong communities were similar ideas, so they were grouped together. Kindness, being kind to all, and inclusivity were alike, so they were grouped together.

Setting an example for others was a stand-alone idea, but it was important to all of us, so it was also incorporated. We kept grouping ideas until they were all in little themed bundles.

STEP FOUR: CREATE YOUR UNIQUE FAMILY VALUES

Then came the fun part! That is when we put it all together. We decided to follow a format similar to an affirmation, but instead of using "I am" statements, we used "We are" statements. For example, our first value was, "We are servant leaders." We came up with that by looking at our grouped themes from step three. The idea of service and leadership showed up in multiple stories. Once we put those two words together, we dug in deeper to describe what it means to us to be a "servant leader." To us, servant leadership is about being kind to everyone. It's about being generous with our resources, setting a good example, and bringing people together.

Those were all ideas and strengths we found embedded in our stories. When we put several of the themes from our stories together, we came up with the statement, "We are servant leaders. We are kind to all and generously share our life's blessings to set a loving example for the like-hearted families we bring together." We continued the process until we had a list of well-defined values for our family.

STEP FIVE: REVISIT AND READJUST.

We had to do that process several times over the course of a few years to get to what we feel is a final product. Our first time through the process, we created four family values. We have since done this exercise a handful more times. Each time, we revised what we created previously and added some new values. Today, we have six family values and feel really good about every word in them. Each time we have a new experience, we see if they fit into our values somewhere, and so far, they have.

With our values complete, Mike had a graphic designer turn them into artwork. We have them hanging over our mantel, and the kids each have a smaller copy in their bedrooms as a reminder of how we want to show up in the world as a family.

WHAT DOES THE FINISHED PRODUCT LOOK LIKE?

Here is our current list of family values to give you an example of the finished product this process can produce. Please don't be discouraged if your first go-around doesn't get you to this point. Remember, it took several revisions to get our family here. We consider this a living document that we revisit from time to time.

- **We are Servant Leaders-** We are kind to all and generously share our life's blessings to set a loving example for the like-hearted families we bring together.

- **We are Playful Adventurers-** We are intuitively open to new possibilities and explore the world together, finding the magic in every moment.

- **We are Transformation Seekers-** We are continually curious how we can individually and collectively be our best and challenge ourselves to live outside our comfort zone.

- **We are Present Visionaries-** We are grateful and grounded in the moment as we co-create a life of abundance, adventure, and authenticity.

- **We are Resilient Warriors-** We are strong, courageous, and swift because we embrace the McCarthy family motto, "Nothing is difficult to the brave and faithful."

- **We are Peaceful Collaborators-** We live in integrity, and through accountability, work together as a team to support each other in achieving our goals.

MCCARTHY FAMILY VALUES

WE INTUITIVELY OPEN TO NEW POSSIBILITIES AND EXPLORE THE WORLD TOGETHER FINDING THE MAGIC IN EVERY MOMENT.

PLAYFUL ADVENTURERS

We are strong, courageous and swift because we embrace our McCarthy family motto: "Nothing is difficult to the brave and faithful"

RESILIENT WARRIORS

WE ARE CONTINUALLY CURIOUS ABOUT HOW WE CAN INDIVIDUALLY AND COLLECTIVELY BE OUR BEST, AND CHALLENGE OURSELVES TO LIVE OUTSIDE OUR COMFORT ZONES.

TRANSFORMATION SEEKERS

WE ARE KIND TO ALL AND GENEROUSLY SHARE OUR LIFE'S BLESSINGS, TO SET A LOVING EXAMPLE FOR THE LIKE-HEARTED FAMILIES WE BRING TOGETHER.

SERVANT LEADERS

PEACEFUL COLLABORATORS

We live in integrity through accountability and work together as a team to support each other in achieving our goals.

we are grateful and grounded in the moment as we co-create a life of abundance, adventure, and authenticity.

PRESENT VISIONARIES

Here are some examples from other families we've taken through this process. Note, they do not all look the same because each family is different. You have different strengths and capabilities, so your finished product will fit your family.

AITCHISON FAMILY

- Growth: We are always learning and looking to improve, even when it's uncomfortable.
- Respect: We treat ourselves and others with love, kindness, and respect.
- Integrity: We are truthful and always do the right thing, no matter what.
- Gratitude: We are grateful and appreciative for all the blessings in our life.
- Attitude: We choose to have a positive attitude in all situations.
- Accountability: We take ownership and responsibility for everything in our life.
- Appreciation: We acknowledge and uplift people with our words and actions.
- Leadership: We stand up and speak out for what we believe in and lead by example.
- Persistence: We overcome all challenges and obstacles by never giving up.
- Love: We unconditionally love, support, and encourage our family and friends.
- Adventure: We play hard and explore with curiosity.

FLEWELLING FAMILY

- Family: Within an abundance of attraction, we are committed to family, well-being, and balance.
- Kindness: We treat ourselves and our bodies with kindness while treating others the way we want to be treated.
- Positivity: We seek to solve challenges with creativity, problem-solving, and enthusiasm.
- Curiosity: We have a strong desire to learn and to play at the highest ability we can.
- Prosperity: We are focused on long-term prosperity and health while enjoying the moment and journey.

VROMAN FAMILY

"FEEL THE BEET" *NOURISHMENT*

Vromans nourish themselves and others. We believe in home-cooked meals that energize our whole being. We respect our environment and connect with nature. We love being barefoot and grounded. We move our bodies in rhythm with the planet. In sync. Connected to our source. We choose to plug in, play, dance, laugh, and sing. We choose to rest, recover, and repeat. We feel the beet.

"ALOHA" *CONNECTION*

Vromans value community. We cherish our friends and love making new ones. Seeing the good in all that surrounds us. We believe in making memories. Experiences over things. Happiness is only real when shared. We smile, snuggle, and hug with love. We quickly forgive, forget, and move forward. We give more than we take.

"AWE, YEAH" *ORIGINALITY*

Vromans love to create. We believe in making things better than we found them. We're deeply interested in learning new things. Feeling boundless in our potential. Learning from our mistakes and making the best of whatever is given to us. Seeking adventure. Creating boldly. Taking healthy risks. Forever feeling a sense of awe, an endless curiosity, and childlike wonder. The world is our canvas, and daily we make art.

BOSTRACK FAMILY

Human Beings vs. Human Doings

- Be Resilient: Practice mindfulness to honor authenticity, adaptability, and perseverance.
- Be Awesome: Discover creative ways to find adventure outside of your comfort zone.
- Be Brave: Courageously step into the best version of yourself daily. Work hard to be intentional and execute on promises to yourself and others.
- Be Kind: Practice compassion, generosity, and use thoughtful words.

MCFARLAND FAMILY

McFarland's Do Hard Things

- We are a team.
- We live a life of adventure.
- We are creators & dream big.
- We always support each other.
- We are active & eat plants.
- Our honesty & ownership will never be punished.

—YOUR TURN—
DISCOVER YOUR FAMILY VALUES

SUPPLIES:

- Your family
- Easel, whiteboard, or wall
- Sticky notes
- Family Values Worksheet or blank paper (you can download additional copies of the worksheet from www.miraclemorning.com/parentsplaybook)
- Pencils, Pens, or Markers

OBJECTIVE:

The objective of this exercise is to create a list of your unique family values. You will discover your family's strengths and capabilities through your personal stories and then use those stories to articulate your family's values, so you can start using them to direct your lives. You have always been teaching your children your values through your actions; now it's time to put them into words to make them even more powerful. It's never too late to do this process with your kids!

To get started, we suggest you set aside a couple of hours when your whole family can be present and won't be distracted. If you have kids under five, allow them to participate as much or as little as they want, but encourage them to be in the room so they can hear the discussions taking place. You can also break this up into multiple sessions if you have kids with a short attention span. We like to do this at a table so everyone can see each other, preferably in a semicircle with everyone facing the easel.

THIS EXERCISE HAS FIVE STEPS:

1. Remember when your family was at their best.
2. Share stories and capture strengths and values.
3. Synthesize themes.
4. Create your unique values.
5. Revisit and readjust.

STEP ONE: REMEMBER WHEN YOUR FAMILY WAS AT THEIR BEST.

Give each family member a piece of paper or use the worksheet provided; set a timer for ten minutes to think and journal or draw about the times your family was at its best. Make a list of your family's greatest moments, challenges you've overcome, the success you've achieved, and adventures you've experienced. Come up with three to five stories about when your family was thriving. The goal is to discover when your family has *already* been at its best. Maybe it's a story about an ancestor or a recent story.

STEP TWO: SHARE STORIES AND CAPTURE STRENGTHS AND VALUES.

In this step, give everyone a pad of sticky notes and a marker. Now that everyone has their stories top of mind, have one conversation around the table. Each member of the family, starting with the youngest, should share *one* of their examples and go around the table until everyone has shared *all* their ideas. If someone has more than others, it's okay. If you have no more to share, move to the next person until all ideas are shared.

This is a time for sharing ideas, and there are no "bad" or "wrong" thoughts. Everyone should feel free to share in this phase. The more stories you share, the more complete your list of values will be. However, you don't want this exercise to take all day, so you may want to limit everyone to three or four stories, maybe less if you have a big family. When it's your turn, feel free to elaborate on *why* you thought your family was at its best in that moment.

As you listen to the stories being shared, write down any words that would describe a strength, quality, or principle you heard in the story. Put one word or idea per sticky note. Think about answering these questions on the sticky notes: what family strengths does this story illustrate? What did you or our family bring to the situation? What principle helped create this moment of family excellence? Capture as many keywords as you can on sticky notes; that will be helpful for the next step.

STEP THREE: SYNTHESIZE THEMES.

Now you should have a bunch of sticky notes with words or pictures on them (or both). Identify themes within the stories and start to organize and group similar ideas together. You should start seeing patterns and main ideas emerge. Those might be the ideas you choose for the titles of your family values. Other ideas will go into creating the definition. Also, look for powerful outlier ideas that might not fit within other themes but are still important to your family.

STEP FOUR: CREATE YOUR UNIQUE FAMILY VALUES.

Take your keywords from step three and come up with distinct and unique family values. Start by creating a one-to-two-word catchy title for each theme, and then write out a sentence definition for each value. You can also add "We are" to the beginning of each title if you would like. Come up with three to six values with a title and a description for each.

STEP FIVE: REVISIT AND READJUST.

Let me remind you, this exercise is not one you will do once and be done forever. The documents you will create in this book are all living documents that will grow and change as you do. So don't feel discouraged if yours doesn't look like ours the first time through. Also, keep in mind that the process itself is what creates the magic. You're free to hang our family values on your wall, but they may not describe *your* family's unique strengths and capacities. Feel free to revisit this exercise again and again until you feel complete and the list of values totally captures your family.

That being said, there comes a point when tinkering with your values will produce diminishing results. When the time you invest in tweaking a word here or there just doesn't produce enough difference to the meaning to make it worth the time, stop. When your values feel "complete enough," that's when you can start using them as a tool to direct your lives.

FAMILY VALUES WORKSHEET

STEP ONE: REMEMBER WHEN YOUR FAMILY WAS AT THEIR BEST.

Make a list of your family's greatest moments, challenges you've overcome, the success you've achieved, or adventures you've experienced. Then take turns sharing them as a family.

_____

_____

_____

_____

STEP TWO: SHARE STORIES AND CAPTURE STRENGTHS AND VALUES.

As you share stories and examples, listen for the strengths, qualities, or principles that helped create those moments of family excellence. (Capture *all* key words on sticky notes)

_____

_____

_____

_____

STEP THREE: SYNTHESIZE THEMES.

Identify themes within the stories and strengths, organize your sticky notes on the flip chart around the key patterns and ideas that emerge. Also, look for powerful outlier ideas that might not fit within other themes but are still important to your family.

_____

_____

_____

_____

STEP FOUR: CREATE YOUR UNIQUE FAMILY VALUES.

Create three (or more) Family Values from the themes and patterns, then for each value, create a one- or two-word catchy title, and write a short description of what it means to live that value.

Example: (We are) one- or two-word title or value, followed by a one to two-sentence description of what it means to live this value so it serves as a guiding principle.

1. (We are) Value: _____   _____:

   Guiding Principle: _____

   _____

2. (We are) Value: _____   _____:

   Guiding Principle: _____

   _____

3. (We are) Value: _____   _____:

   Guiding Principle: _____

   _____

4. (We are) Value: _____   _____:

   Guiding Principle: _____

   _____

5. (We are) Value: _____   _____:

   Guiding Principle: _____

   _____

6. (We are) Value: _____   _____:

   Guiding Principle: _____

   _____

EXERCISE FOUR: THE S.T.A.R.R. SYSTEM

*"Our children are counting on us
to provide two things: consistency and structure.
Children need parents who say what they mean,
mean what they say, and do what they say they are going to do."*

—Barbara Coloroso, *bestselling parenting author of Kids are Worth it!*

WHY IS IT IMPORTANT?

Consistency is not something that comes easily to me. My whole life, I've had to create strategies and systems to keep me on track. In school, I had a planner that I lived by. I had to physically write things down to remember them. To this day, I still prefer to put pencil to paper, and I also have a digital calendar that sends me reminders of my most important tasks. If it's not on my calendar, it doesn't exist. As someone who enjoys variety and values flexibility, I need all the tools I can find to help me stay consistent.

All the parenting books I've ever read stress how important consistency and structure are in making kids feel safe and secure. That's pretty easy to do when everyone is calm, but in a moment when there could be tension, it becomes more difficult. Like many families today, we struggled with how to create boundaries around our kids' screen time. We hated that it had become a daily battleground. We also wanted to have a way for our kids to earn money and learn some lessons around financial literacy. We wanted our kids to understand what actions would be helpful for them to do to contribute to the family. We wanted to reward those behaviors and build the habit of tracking them early in life. That is still a tough habit for me, and I didn't want them to learn the hard way as an adult.

Before creating the S.T.A.R.R. system, we gave our kids an allowance, but we realized it wasn't teaching the lessons we wanted them to learn about money in the real world. For the most part, you don't just get money for doing nothing. We wanted to teach them about creating a simple balance sheet and that, one way or another, you must do some work to earn money. We wanted them to learn about opportunity cost—when you say "yes" to something, you are saying "no" to something else. We wanted to build a system that rewarded hard work, but if they only did the bare minimum, they would feel what it's like to live paycheck to paycheck or even go into debt. That's not an area that is covered in school and is largely left to the parents to teach at home. Considering that most American households are in debt, statistically speaking, many don't have the tools to teach these skills at home.

We wanted to create a system that would help us be consistent as parents while also using positive reinforcement—a system that rewards the kids for doing the things we want them to do and where they could be in control of how they use those rewards to earn the things they want. We wanted them to have some autonomy over their screen use and allowance. So, we created a system that combines it all and called it the S.T.A.R.R. system. We love acronyms, and this one stands for Screen Time, Allowance, Responsibilities, and Rewards.

As we always do, we included our kids in creating the system because we understand their input is directly correlated to their buy-in. They helped us create a list of rewards they'd like to earn, responsibilities they felt they could complete independently, and how many S.T.A.R.R.s they would earn or spend. We put it all into a Google Sheet, printed it out, and laminated it. Each evening before bed, they go through their charts, tally up all the S.T.A.R.R.s they earned, and subtract all the S.T.A.R.R.s they spent, creating a simple daily balance sheet.

We like this system because it focuses on positive reinforcement instead of punishment. *Positive reinforcement* is defined as "the act of rewarding a positive behavior in order to encourage it to happen again in the future." All the responsibilities on the chart are things we'd like them to do, such as chores around the house, habits we'd like them to develop, and things like *getting caught living the family values* and *writing someone a nice note*. We do not take any S.T.A.R.R.s away for bad behavior, but they can lose all their S.T.A.R.R.s if they violate our family screen-time contract (more on that in the next exercise). They can use their S.T.A.R.R.s to "buy" rewards. At first, we had a long list of rewards, but as we've gone through new iterations, we have whittled it down to three—cash, screen time, and sweet treats.

This system gives the kids more autonomy and has prevented a lot of nagging on our part. Now, allowance is up to them. They choose when they want to cash in S.T.A.R.R.s for money. When they get money, they also decide if it's for spending, saving, or sharing. We've always encouraged them to pay themselves first: save 10%, share 10% with a charity of their choice, and then keep the rest for spending. However, it's up to them where they put the money. The kids have choices in this system, and they make tradeoffs. If they do what we'd like them to do, they will have enough S.T.A.R.R.s in their account to enjoy screen time *and* receive some spending money *and* have a sweet treat. If they don't do those things, they will not. If they forget to track their responsibilities for the day but use screen time, they don't earn anything but still get charged for the screen time, so they can actually go into debt. We haven't allowed them to borrow S.T.A.R.R.s yet, but this can be a future lesson on how credit and interest work.

HOW DID WE DO IT?

To create the first draft, we sat the kids down at one of our family meetings and got out our easel, sticky notes, and markers. We told them we wanted to try out a system where they could earn even more allowance than they were currently. We told them they'd earn McCarthy S.T.A.R.R.s and be able to trade them in for different rewards. The kids liked the idea of unlimited allowance and rewards, so we thought we'd start there.

We had them write or draw on their sticky notes the different rewards they'd like to earn and how many S.T.A.R.R.s they believed each one was worth.

They put things like money, screen time, later bedtime, family movie, sleepover at a friend's house, playdates, dessert, trip to the store, and dinner out.

Then we asked them what they thought they could do around the house to help out and earn those rewards and how many S.T.A.R.R.s they believed it to be worth. That list included personal hygiene actions like brushing teeth, flossing, brushing hair, showering, or bathing, and cutting fingernails and toenails. It also included habits we'd like them to develop like C.H.A.R.M.S., getting caught living the family values, and writing notes to people.

The majority of the list is chores, or as we like to call them, "family contributions." Those range from feeding the dog to helping with laundry and meals, taking out the trash, and unloading the dishwasher. It also includes getting a good grade at school.

When we were done with this exercise, we had two sections on the wall with sticky notes covering each. One section listed all the rewards they would like to be able to earn, and the other section listed all the things they would do to earn S.T.A.R.R.s. Once we knew what they valued for each section, we negotiated the final S.T.A.R.R. value for each activity.

Since the introduction of this system, our kids' charts have been identical, but we have toyed with the idea of customizing them since Tyler is four years older and more physically capable than his sister for certain items. Our thinking has been that most of the items are pretty equal opportunity, so it comes down to motivation, and if Tyler does more, he should earn more. However, that will be a family decision.

Also, when we started, we wanted our kids to have some S.T.A.R.R.s that were *really* easy to earn so they wouldn't dig themselves into a hole right off the bat. We have since removed some things that are now habits for our kids and no longer need to be rewarded. For example, on our first iteration, they could earn a S.T.A.R.R. for eating meals without complaining. They were literally earning three S.T.A.R.R.s a day just for eating. Luckily, that bad habit was soon corrected, and they both were consistently eating peacefully, so we decided as a family that we no longer needed that one on the chart.

These charts have helped open up conversations with our kids and helped our family stay focused on the things we have identified to be important. At one point, Tyler asked if he could get more than one S.T.A.R.R. if he brushed his teeth or hair more than once a day. That created a great clarifying conversation about the expectations. Without this tracking system in place, Mike and I may not have realized our kids were only brushing their teeth once a day.

By having it all in a checklist, Mike and I don't have to use additional energy reminding the kids what we'd like them to do. It's already written out for them. There are no surprises. The expectations are clear. The rewards are set, and the kids know how many S.T.A.R.R.s they need to buy them. There are fewer negotiations and fewer fights over screen time.

WHAT DOES THE FINISHED PRODUCT LOOK LIKE?

Here is what our current chart looks like, so you have an example. It is a two-sided laminated checklist. On the front are all the possible ways to earn S.T.A.R.R.s, and on the back are ways to spend S.T.A.R.R.s along with a habit tracker for their C.H.A.R.M.S. We had ours laminated, and the kids use wet-erase markers to mark it up each day. At the end of the week, I track their S.T.A.R.R.s in a Google Sheet on my computer so we could look back at trends if we wanted to and have a running record. Then, they erase their marks and start over, keeping the S.T.A.R.R.s they earned that week.

McCarthy Starrs

EARN S.T.A.R.R.S.

STARTING BALANCE _____

TASK	S	M	T	W	TH	F	S
GENERAL STARRS							
Make your Bed (1)	◯	◯	◯	◯	◯	◯	◯
Family Hug (1)	◯	◯	◯	◯	◯	◯	◯
Complete Miracle Morning CHARMS (1)	◯	◯	◯	◯	◯	◯	◯
Make/Pack your own lunch (2)	◯	◯	◯	◯	◯	◯	◯
Feed Bodhi/take Bodhi out (1)	◯	◯	◯	◯	◯	◯	◯
Help Cook/Prepare a Meal (2)	◯	◯	◯	◯	◯	◯	◯
Try a new food (1)	◯	◯	◯	◯	◯	◯	◯
15 mins of Exercise (not including CHARMS) (1)	◯	◯	◯	◯	◯	◯	◯
Shower/Bath (2)	◯	◯	◯	◯	◯	◯	◯
Cut Finger or Toe Nails (1)	◯	◯	◯	◯	◯	◯	◯
Brush Hair/teeth/floss (1)	◯	◯	◯	◯	◯	◯	◯
DOING GOOD							
Get "caught" living Family Values (2)	◯	◯	◯	◯	◯	◯	◯
Write a Thank You or Note to someone (2)	◯	◯	◯	◯	◯	◯	◯
Donate $20 (10)	◯	◯	◯	◯	◯	◯	◯
Family Dream Session or Tutor Call (1)	◯	◯	◯	◯	◯	◯	◯
Get an "A" at school (1)	◯	◯	◯	◯	◯	◯	◯
OTHER FAMILY CONTRIBUTIONS							
Take trash to garage (1)	◯	◯	◯	◯	◯	◯	◯
Take trash to street/bring in cans (2)	◯	◯	◯	◯	◯	◯	◯
Un/load Dishwasher/put dishes away (2)	◯	◯	◯	◯	◯	◯	◯
Help with Laundry (1)	◯	◯	◯	◯	◯	◯	◯
Tally your stars (1)	◯	◯	◯	◯	◯	◯	◯

DAILY TOTAL _____

MINUS INVESTMENT _____

DAILY NET _____

YOUR TURN: CREATE YOUR S.T.A.R.R. SYSTEM SUPPLIES:

- Your family
- S.T.A.R.R. Chart Worksheet (you can download additional copies of this worksheet from www.miraclemorning.com/parentsplaybook)
- Sticky notes
- Markers
- Easel, wall, or large whiteboard
- Volunteer to create the Google Sheet

OBJECTIVE:

By the end of this exercise, you should have your own unique S.T.A.R.R. accountability chart that lists responsibilities the kids can handle independently and rewards they can earn. It's up to the family what those responsibilities and rewards are and if each child has an individual chart with personal responsibilities and rewards or if each child has an identical chart. You can always start out with the same charts for everyone and individualize them when you revisit it after trying it for a while.

THIS EXERCISE HAS SIX STEPS:

1. Identify rewards and the S.T.A.R.R. value.
2. Identify responsibilities and the S.T.A.R.R. value.
3. Have the decisions discussion.
4. Create your chart.
5. Follow through.
6. Revisit and revise.

STEP ONE: IDENTIFY REWARDS.

Each person in the family gets a stack of sticky notes and a marker. Write or draw out the type of rewards you'd like to earn and the suggested S.T.A.R.R. value. Only include one idea per sticky note. Think about things that would motivate you to work hard. Is it money, the promise of a pizza night, special time with Mom or Dad, playdates with friends, screen time, or sweet treats? This is the time to generate as many ideas as you can. Set a timer for five to ten minutes and get as many ideas onto sticky notes as you can. As you write them out, place your sticky note up on the wall and say it out loud.

STEP TWO: IDENTIFY RESPONSIBILITIES.

Now, it's time to repeat that process with responsibilities. Take another five to ten minutes and brainstorm as many chores or "family contributions" that you can think of. What are things you currently do around the house that you'd like to get credit for? Parents, what are some jobs you'd love some help with around the house? Are there other behaviors or habits you'd like to develop that can be added here? Again, the point is to generate as many ideas as you can and suggest a S.T.A.R.R value for each to be negotiated later. Don't edit or discuss any answers yet. After you write it down, put the sticky note up on the easel and say it out loud.

STEP THREE: DECISIONS DISCUSSIONS.

Now that all the ideas are out of our heads, down on sticky notes, and up where everyone can see them, it's time to make some decisions. Which ideas stay and which go? Negotiate how many S.T.A.R.R.s can each responsibility earn. How much should each reward cost? Can S.T.A.R.R.s be borrowed like credit? If so, do you want to charge interest? How much? Do you want to individualize the charts for each child or keep them all the same? Do older kids earn more or less S.T.A.R.R.s for the same contribution as a younger sibling? For younger children, do you want to use pictures instead of words?

STEP FOUR: CREATE YOUR CHART.

It's time to put it all together and decide how your chart is going to look. Do you have an artist in the family who would like to create it? Maybe someone in the family is tech-savvy and wants to make it into a spreadsheet. In my experience, the easier you make it, the sooner you can start using it.

Also, remember that you will probably need to update it periodically, so having a digital version you can easily change and reprint may be the way to go. We made a simple spreadsheet, printed it out, and had it laminated. That way, we could use wet-erase markers to track it on a weekly basis and wipe it clean to use it again.

STEP FIVE: FOLLOW THROUGH.

When and how will you total your family's S.T.A.R.R.s daily and review each kid's progress? This step may seem obvious, but you might be surprised how many people create a system and then don't use it! You can always tweak it if something isn't working, but you won't know that until you start and give it a try. It could easily be added to your bedtime ritual so that it is completed at the end of each day.

STEP SIX: REVISIT AND REVISE.

After a couple of weeks, you may notice that some rewards or responsibilities need to be added or removed. You may want to incentivize certain behaviors by making them worth more S.T.A.R.R.s. Maybe the kids think it's too hard to earn the rewards they want and have lost motivation, or maybe it's too easy, and they haven't been helping out like you would have wanted and need to charge more for their rewards.

When changes are made, there should be another family discussion. Top-down management is bad for motivation, so make sure the kids have a say in the decisions, so they are fully bought into them. Everyone can share their feedback about how it's going and propose any changes they'd like to make.

S.T.A.R.R. CHART WORKSHEET

STEP ONE: IDENTIFY REWARDS.

Write or draw out the type of rewards you'd like to earn and the suggested S.T.A.R.R. value for each reward.

_____

_____

_____

_____

STEP TWO: IDENTIFY RESPONSIBILITIES.

Brainstorm as many chores or "family contributions" that you can think of. What are things you currently do around the house that you'd like to get credit for? Parents, what are some jobs you'd love some help with around the house? Are there other behaviors or habits you'd like to develop that can be added here?

_____

_____

_____

STEP THREE: DECISIONS DISCUSSION.

It's time to make some decisions. Which ideas stay and which go? Negotiate S.T.A.R.R.s values for each responsibility and reward?

_____

_____

_____

_____

STEP FOUR: CREATE YOUR CHART.

What format will you use for your tracker to total and balance your S.T.A.R.R.s each day? You can use a spreadsheet, a laminated and printed worksheet, a custom chart, a combination of printed and electronic trackers, or whatever approach works best for you.

_____

_____

_____

_____

STEP FIVE: FOLLOW THROUGH.

When and how will you total your family's S.T.A.R.R.s daily and review each child's progress?

_____

_____

_____

_____

EXERCISE FIVE:
YOUR FAMILY SCREEN-TIME CONTRACT

WHY IS IT IMPORTANT?

As a kid growing up in the '80s, I felt blessed to be one of the last generations to enjoy a fairly screen-free childhood. Yes, I had a TV, but there were only a handful of channels, and VHS tapes were kind of crappy compared to today's graphics. We got a Nintendo when I was in elementary school, but I had little interest in it. We got a computer when I was in middle school, and I remember learning to use floppy disks and playing Oregon Trail in *computer lab* at school. When I was in high school, AOL was all the rage, and I got my first email address, which I never checked. When I got my driver's license at sixteen, I also got a flip phone "in case of an emergency." In college, AOL Instant Messages were how all my friends communicated. I got a Facebook account my senior year of college and didn't get my first smartphone until after I was married. I got to grow up alongside technology and am forever grateful my "awkward years" are only captured in photographs buried in my parent's attic and not plastered all over the internet.

Tyler was born in 2009. The iPad came out in 2010, and Mike and I were early adopters. As young parents who had grown up alongside technology, we saw no harm in handing it to our baby. There were no studies out on the dangers to children's brain development back then. If we wanted some extra time to chat at a restaurant after Tyler was done eating, we simply handed him a device, and he would happily sit there for as long as we'd let him have the device. This new technology was so intuitive to use that a baby could do it... literally! That was not the technology of my youth. We started noticing Tyler's behavior deteriorate anytime we took the iPad away from him, and we knew we had to make some changes.

In 2014, Nick Bilton wrote an article for *The New York Times* about Steve Jobs and other tech CEOs limiting their children's access to the devices and apps they created. He wrote, "I never asked Mr. Jobs what his children did instead of using the gadgets he built, so I reached out to Walter Isaacson, the author of *Steve Jobs*, who spent a lot of time at their home. Every evening, Steve made a point of having dinner at the big, long table in their kitchen, discussing books and history and a variety of things," he said. "No one ever pulled out an iPad or computer. The kids did not seem addicted at all to devices." Clearly, they knew something the rest of us didn't.

I also found the movie *The Social Dilemma* to be very eye-opening into the addictive nature of social media platforms and how they use human psychology to keep us scrolling much longer than we need or even want to. Teenage mental health problems and suicide rates are on the rise and strongly correlates with heavy technology use.

According to the CDC, kids aged eight to ten spend, on average, six hours daily in front of a screen just for entertainment purposes. That doesn't even include the time they spend on a computer or iPad at school or for homework. Kids eleven to fourteen spend an average of nine hours a day being entertained, and in ages fifteen to eighteen, it drops to seven-and-a-half hours. Sadly, it's not just the kids that are overindulging. Many parents also struggle to impose healthy limits for themselves. According to the Kaiser Family Foundation, the average adult spends over eleven hours per day behind a screen. Technology is a wonderful tool in many ways. However, we need to acknowledge that it also has risks. Discuss them as a family and set healthy boundaries, not just for the kids, but for ourselves too.

It's an issue that is up to families to solve at home. As parents, we need to model healthy behavior for our kids. It's up to us to set time limits and appropriate boundaries around the content our kids are consuming. It's up to us to protect media-free times and areas in our homes. It's our job to teach our kids etiquette when it comes to digital devices and how to be safe online. It's up to us to decide what gaming platforms and games are allowed into our homes. We need to decide when it's okay to give our kids a cell phone. We are the first generation of parents that haswho have had to deal with this issue, and we get to lead the way for our children.

HOW DID WE DO IT?

When we started the S.T.A. R. R. chart system, we limited our kids to "buying" two hours of screen time a day that they were supposed to self-manage. They could use any device they wanted and could break it up any way they saw fit and were in charge of setting a timer to track it. After about a week, we realized they were not quite mature enough to have so much freedom. They constantly forgot to set timers and almost daily lost track of how much screen time they had used. I had read about the concept of a "screen-time contract" and thought it could be the solution for us.

True to our values, we decided that too needed to be a collaborative effort, so we sat the kids down and told them our frustrations. They were frustrated because they felt like our reactions to their oversights were not very consistent. Sometimes we overreacted if we were in a bad mood, and sometimes we overlooked it altogether if we were tired and didn't feel like fighting with them. I seemingly had different rules than Mike, and no one could remember the rules we thought we had set. The S.T.A. R. R. chart was helping in other areas, but it did not fully solve the screen time battles.

The answer seemed so simple—let's write out the rules, and we'll all agree to them. We found that the more specific they were, the less opportunity there was to find loopholes in the document. We also found that defining things cut down on ambiguous expectations. We also wanted to build in a loophole for ourselves for days when we were tired and needed a little family time staring at a screen. If we were too rigid, it would suck out all the joy of screen time, but if we were too lenient, the document would mean nothing, and it wouldn't solve any of the challenges we were experiencing.

We had to find the right balance of flexibility and structure. I like to think of it as bumper bowling. The contract acts as the bumpers. The bumpers are there to increase the odds of successfully knocking down some pins. The contract makes it easier for everyone to be on the same page about the rules. Everyone has a say in them, and everyone agrees to them ahead of time. Now, when anyone bumps against one of the rules, the course of action is already laid out, and they gently put us back on track. With practice, we all become more skilled, and the ball stays on course right down the middle. Eventually, we don't really need the bumpers anymore because we have mastered the basics.

This, too, is a living document and may need revisiting and updating. Our kids are still fairly young. Tyler is twelve, and Ember is eight. Tyler has recently been bugging us to get his own cell phone. Many of his classmates have cell phones, and even his younger cousin just got one. To buy ourselves some time, we said we needed to think about it. I did some quick research and found some prepaid phones he could probably afford, but it was not easy to figure out how much it would cost on an ongoing basis. Mike and I are not necessarily opposed to him getting a cell phone, but we don't see any real legitimate *need* for him to have one either.

We told him that if he does the research to find a phone he can afford to pay for by himself and keep up with the payments, he could get one.

I like that approach because we're not flat-out saying, "no," and he has to be motivated to use some of his daily screen time to do the research to present to us. That puts the ball in his court. It's his choice to decide if a cell phone is worth the money he would have to shell out for it.

So far, he hasn't presented us with anything. When he does get a cell phone, it may not come with a contract from the cell phone company, but it will definitely come with a contract from Mom and Dad.

Your kids may not like this screen-time contract, but I believe it's our duty as parents to set healthy boundaries, and deep down, our kids appreciate knowing they are safe and have a voice in important decisions.

Our original document only had rules for the kids, but Tyler so lovingly pointed out that we too could do better. We decided to revise our contract to add some family rules Mike and I also committed to following. Mainly, they are the "device-free zones" in our home, including bedrooms and protected family times (dinner, family meetings, and movie nights). Mike and I do not have a TV in our bedroom, and neither do our kids. The whole family has committed to charging all our devices outside our bedrooms, except our Echo Dots. Instead of watching TV to go to sleep, we listen to an audiobook, a guided meditation, soft music, or nature sounds on Alexa with a sleep timer. We know we have to lead by example, so we made this commitment as a family.

WHAT DOES THE FINISHED PRODUCT LOOK LIKE?

Here is our current screen-time contract for you to have as an example. Again, I want to remind you that the magic of these documents lies in the creation process. Our screen-time contract will not be as powerful for your family as the one you create together as a family. Also, having everyone sign the document makes it more official. When signing a legal document, it signifies that the signing party has read the document, understands the contents, and consents to the stipulations of the contract. Here, we are doing the same thing.

MCCARTHY FAMILY SCREEN-TIME CONTRACT

- I agree to set a timer when I'm using screen time and agree to ask permission to use another timer after 30 minutes. I will mark it off on my S.T.A.R.R. chart before starting a new timer, so I don't lose track.

- If I fail to set a timer *or* the timer fails, I will lose the remainder of my screen time that day, or an hour the next day if it was the last timer.

- On school days, I agree to use only one hour of screen time, outside of school hours, unless I get permission from Mom and/or Dad to use more and have the S.T.A.R.R.s to buy more time.

- On weekends or school breaks, I am allowed three hours of screen time daily. On travel days, additional screen time is at the discretion of Mom and/or Dad.

- When I'm at a friend's house, I will respect their family's rules and follow our family's values. Mom and Dad will not enforce our limits when I'm in the care of others outside our home and will trust me to do the right thing.

- Noneducational screen time will cost me 1 S.T.A.R.R. for 10 minutes or 3 S.T.A.R.R.s for 30 minutes. Educational/work screen time will not cost any S.T.A.R.R.s but will be counted in my time total. Educational/work screen time is defined as parent-approved documentaries, creating or editing videos, and any learning programs used at school (Khan, Dream Box, Spelling Classroom, etc.). Watching YouTube videos does not count as educational screen time (even if I happen to learn something).

- I agree to get off my device when the timer is done within five minutes. If I fail to do so, I will lose 30 minutes that day and 30 minutes the next day or an hour the next day if it's on my last timer.

- I agree to get Mom and/or Dad's approval before posting anything to YouTube or anywhere else on the internet. If I fail to get approval, I will lose my screen time for one week. Mom and Dad agree to get your permission before posting any photos or videos of you on the internet.

- I agree that I will show Mom and/or Dad my Facebook Messenger kids/ text messages if they request to see them. If there is anything inappropriate found, I will lose my screen time for one week.

- If I'm caught using screen time when I'm not supposed to (before C.H.A.R.M.S., after 8 p.m., or after I've used my allotted time that day) without permission or I'm found out to be lying about my screen time use, I will receive a warning. On a second offense, my S.T.A.R.R.s will go to zero. On a third offense, I will lose all my S.T.A.R.R.s and the device for 1 week.

- I agree to complete my Miracle Morning before I can enjoy screen time for entertainment, and Mom and Dad do, too. I can use a device as a tool to help complete my Miracle Morning.

- Screen time enjoyed as a family will not count toward my screen time limit.

- Bedrooms, family meals, family dream sessions, family board meetings, and family movie nights are device-free zones for everyone, except for emergency communications.

- Audiobooks do not count as screen time and may be enjoyed without limits, except after 9 p.m. I agree to set a sleep timer if I want to listen at bedtime. If I forget, I will be forgiven and will try to remember better next time.

Signed:

Lindsay McCarthy   *Lindsay McCarthy*   Mike McCarthy   *Mike McCarthy*

Tyler McCarthy   *Tyler McCarthy*   Ember McCarthy   *Ember McCarthy*

—YOUR TURN—
CREATE YOUR FAMILY
SCREEN TIME CONTRACT

SUPPLIES:

- Your family

- Screen Time Contract Worksheet or paper—one sheet per person (you can download additional copies of this worksheet from www.miraclemorning.com/parentsplaybook)

- Something to write with—one per person

- Volunteer to type it up at the end

- Pen to sign it

OBJECTIVE:

The goal of this exercise is to get on the same page and create your family screen-time contract. This exercise will help you do some upfront thinking and decision-making so, in the moment, the parents can be consistent and fair when it comes to screen time violations. It's also about parents leading by example.

This exercise has six steps:

1. Reflect on current screen time rules.
2. Share reflections.
3. Negotiate the contract.
4. Sign the contract.
5. Follow through.
6. Revisit and readjust.

STEP ONE: REFLECT ON CURRENT SCREEN TIME RULES.

Set a timer for ten to fifteen minutes. Each family member should reflect on your current screen time use and rules (if you have any) and write or draw your answers to the following questions:

- What is working with our current rules?

- What is causing frustration in the family around electronic devices?

- What time should our devices go to bed? Should it be the same time for everyone in the family?

- Should the rules be the same on school days versus weekends and breaks? What about during travel?

- What are things I enjoy doing on my devices? How can it be used as a tool or to create?

- What are some things I enjoy doing off screens?

- Are there places in our home or specific family times that devices should not be allowed at all? For example, in the bedrooms or during dinner.

- Should we have a designated charging area in our home? If so, where would be a good place?

- Are there certain things I think need to be accomplished before using screens for entertainment?

- Is there an age that's too young to be on the internet, have social media accounts, a YouTube account, download certain apps, or have a cell phone?

- Who should pay for the cell phone and service?

- How will we keep passwords safe and organized?

- Are there any rules I think are unfair? Why?

- What specific actions should happen if this contract is broken?

- I would love to see Mom and Dad lead by example by...

STEP TWO: SHARE REFLECTIONS.

Now, it's time to share your answers. This is not a time to argue. It's a time to seek understanding and listen to each other. Go around the circle and let each person share their thoughts without interruption. Have one person record the ideas.

STEP THREE: NEGOTIATE THE CONTRACT.

Now, it's time to come together and agree on some boundaries. Whoever wants to be the secretary can start by writing down any rules that are mutually agreed upon. Keep going until you have a good list. Remember, this is an experiment. Agree to give the rules a try for a while and know that they can be revised later. (See Step Six.)

STEP FOUR: WRITE AND SIGN THE CONTRACT.

Once you've hashed out the details, it's time to write out and print your contract and sign it to signify that you have read the contents of the document, understand the contents, and consent to the stipulations of the contract.

STEP FIVE: FOLLOW THROUGH.

This may be the hardest step, but without it, this contract means nothing. As parents, our job is to enforce the rules. Our kids' job is to test our boundaries, and trust me; they will. You've done the hard part of hashing out the rules, so now is the time to reap the benefits and follow through with any consequences you outlined in the contract. Your kids will be mad when they break the rules, and you enforce them, but over time, they shift their anger from you to themselves. Once they understand you will enforce the rules, they aren't as mad at *you* as they are at the rules themselves, which they helped create. Eventually, they must start taking personal responsibility. They know the rules and that they will be enforced, so they can only blame themselves for any consequences.

STEP SIX: REVISIT AND REVISE.

Contracts are binding, but they can still be revised. After at least a week of using the new contract, pause to reflect on how it's going. Was there something you left out the first time? Is there a particular rule that needs to be defined more clearly? Is there a loophole that needs to be synced up? Bring up your concerns during a family meeting, and discuss win-win solutions.

SCREEN-TIME CONTRACT WORKSHEET

STEP ONE: REFLECT ON CURRENT SCREEN TIME RULES.

Set a timer for ten to fifteen minutes. Each family member should reflect on their current screen time use and rules (if they have any) and write or draw their answers to the following questions:

1. What's working with our current rules?

_____

_____

2. What is causing frustration in the family around electronic devices?

_____

_____

3. What time should our devices go to bed? Should it be the same time for everyone in the family? Should the rules be the same on school days versus weekends and breaks? What about during travel?

_____

_____

4. What are things I enjoy doing on my devices? How can it be used as a tool or to create?

_____

_____

5. What are some things I enjoy doing off screens?

6. Are there places in our home or specific family times devices should not be allowed at all? For example, in bedrooms or during dinner.

7. Should we have a designated charging area in our home? If so, where would be a good place?

8. Are there certain things I think need to be accomplished before using screens for entertainment?

9. Is there an age that's too young to be on the internet, have social media accounts, a YouTube account, download certain apps, or have a cell phone?

10. Who should pay for the cell phone and service?

_____

_____

11. How will we keep passwords safe and organized?

_____

_____

12. Are there any rules I think are unfair? Why?

_____

_____

13. What specific actions should happen if this contract is broken?

_____

_____

14. I would love to see Mom and Dad lead by example by...

_____

_____

STEP TWO: SHARE REFLECTIONS.

Go around the circle and let each person share their thoughts without interruption. Have one person record the ideas.

STEP THREE: NEGOTIATE THE CONTRACT.

Now it's time to come together and agree on some boundaries.

# of hours per school day allowed: _____

# of hours per day allowed on weekends: _____

How screen time will be tracked: _____

Penalties for not tracking screen time: _____

What must be completed before screen time can be used: _____

What times of day can screens be used: _____

# of S.T.A.R.R.s for 1 hour of entertainment screen time: _____

# of S.T.A.R.R.s for 1 hour of educational screen time: _____

Where are screens permitted to be used: _____

Where are screens *not* permitted to be used: _____

Additional rules: _____

_____

_____

STEP FOUR: WRITE AND SIGN THE CONTRACT.

Once you've hashed out the details, it's time to write out and print your contract and sign it to signify that you have read the contents of the document, understand the contents, and consent to the stipulations of the contract.

STEP FIVE: FOLLOW THROUGH.

This may be the hardest step, but without it, this contract means nothing. As parents, our job is to enforce the rules. You've done the hard part of hashing out the rules, so now is the time to reap the benefits and follow through with any consequences you outlined in the contract. How will you enforce the rules that have been agreed to in your screen time contact?

_____

_____

EXERCISE SIX: YOUR FAMILY GOALS

"What you get by achieving your goals is not as important as what you become by achieving your goals."

—Henry David Thoreau, American author and philosopher

WHY IS IT IMPORTANT?

Goal setting is a foundational practice, and many schools only gloss over it in their curriculum if they touch on it at all. The connection between setting goals and creating success is well documented. If you search goal setting on the internet, you will find millions of articles and thousands of books on the topic. You will also find a slew of statistics that the vast majority of Americans do not have *any* written goals.

Mike is the cofounder of a group called GoBundance. It's "The Tribe for healthy, wealthy, generous men and women who choose to live epic lives." *Everyone* in that group is successful in business, has written goals and a plan for achieving them. Success is not easy, but it's also not complicated.

Good goal setting is all about getting clear about what's important to you and taking steps in the right direction to achieve your vision. The more specific you can be about your goal, the better. If it's something you can measure, that makes it easier to track. If it's really big, it's a good idea to break it down into smaller pieces. Attaching a deadline or timeframe to your goal helps to keep you motivated and focused. Goals give our lives direction, and accomplishing them gives our lives meaning.

Growing up, I learned about S.M.A.R.T. goals, and apparently, since then, two more letters have been added, which I think are helpful, making the new acronym, S.M.A.R.T.E.R. It stands for S pecific, M easurable, A chievable, R elevant, T ime Bound, E valuate, and R eadjust.

In Greg McKeown's book *Effortless*, he suggests an approach for getting more *specific* about a goal. Let's say you have a vague goal to spend more time with your kids. He suggests asking the question, "What does done look like?" to gain more clarity. In our example, "done" may look like setting aside twenty minutes after dinner to take a walk with your kids. Or it may be scheduling what our friend, Jim Shelis, calls a "family board meeting" with each of your children once a quarter.

That is a one-on-one date with your children where they pick the activity, and no electronics are allowed. Or making family dinner a priority at least five nights a week. The more specific we can be about what we really want, the less inertia we have to overcome to make it a reality.

I will admit not *all* my goals are truly *measurable*, but for the most part, you can make any goal measurable when you do step one and define it in such a way that you can track your progress. If your vague goal is to exercise more, "done" may look like run five miles per week, lift weights twice per week, and do one hour of yoga once per week. Those are all activities you can track to measure your progress. James Clear, the author of *Atomic Habits*, says this about tracking. "The trick is to realize that counting, measuring, and tracking is not about the result. It's about the system, not the goal. Measure from a place of curiosity. Measure to discover, to find out, to understand." If you're new to goal setting, I highly recommend you *do* track your goals. It will give you data, create awareness, and keep you focused on doing what you said is important.

In his book, *The Long View*, Matthew Kelly wrote, "Most people overestimate what they can do in a day and underestimate what they can do in a month. We overestimate what we can do in a year and underestimate what we can accomplish in a decade." I agree with him. We often hold back from dreaming big for the long-term future while we are simultaneously disillusioned by how much is *achievable* in twenty-four hours. We tend to get sidetracked easily by another's priorities instead of staying laser-focused on our goals. We can achieve anything we want in life when we are clear about what we want and we take steps regularly to move closer to that reality. So, dream big for the long term, and make small steps daily to get yourself there.

Setting *relevant* goals simply means they should align with the family values you recently outlined and get you closer to living the life of your dreams. You have to know the "why" behind the goal. For example, one of our values is "We are Playful Adventurers—We are intuitively open to new possibilities and explore the world together, finding the magic in every moment." To align with that value, one of our goals is to visit all fifty states before our kids are eighteen. We love to travel, and we love variety, so we set that goal to help us plan and accomplish the things we say are important to us.

If goals are not *time-bound*, there is no urgency to achieve them. If you have a goal that will take you all year, you have to break it down into smaller pieces so you can monitor your progress. When you have a big goal, like to launch a book this year, you have to break it down into smaller steps: (1) have the rough draft done by such-and-such a date, (2) have it to the editor by this date, (3) have the cover done by this date, etc. Once everything has a specific date attached, it's easy to just follow the laid-out plan to success.

The next two steps are to *evaluate* and *readjust* your goals. Periodically, we realize that a goal we set at the beginning of the year is not achievable or realistic, and we need to course-correct. For example, last year, we were supposed to cross Hawaii and Alaska off our list of states, but Covid-19 hit, and the world shut down. It was simply not possible to make it on those trips. We had to readjust our goals and, instead, explore closer to home. It doesn't mean you're quitting if you find your goal was out of reach or you simply changed your mind and want to replace it with something more meaningful.

HOW DID WE DO IT?

In GoBundance, they have six pillars that guide their goals: Age-Defying Health, Authentic Relationships, Bucket List Adventures, Extreme Accountability, Genuine Contribution, and Horizontal Income. We decided to use those categories but rename them to make them more family-friendly. We decided to set family goals in the following areas: Healthy Habits, Authentic Relationships, Making Memories, Honoring Commitments, Genuine Contribution, and Financial Literacy.

We gathered around the kitchen table, and we told the kids we wanted to set some goals for our family, and we wanted them to set a couple of individual goals too. Mike and I usually set one or two big goals for the year and smaller goals in each of the above categories. The family goals are something everyone is working on together, and we hold each other accountable. We went through each category, explained what it meant, and asked their opinion on what we wanted to set as our collective goals.

I played secretary, we went through each category, and I wrote down all the ideas. The first time through, we were trying to gather as many ideas as possible, so there were no "bad" ideas, and I wrote everything down.

We told the kids Healthy Habits are the things we do to keep our bodies healthy, like exercising, eating healthy foods, doing preventative care, visiting the dentist, and getting a physical. I wrote down our ideas: hike, paddleboard, bike, ski, snowboard, yoga, walk Bodhi, everyone gets a yearly physical and visits the dentist twice, eat dinner together five times a week, and eat one vegetarian meal per week together.

Next was Authentic Relationships. We told the kids this category was about building our relationships with friends, family, and each other. We asked what things we wanted to do as a family to create shared experiences.

Here are some of the ideas:

- Go to church together.
- Hold "Family Board Meetings."
- Have family game nights.
- Host movie nights.
- FaceTime with grandparents.
- Listen to the same books.
- Cook dinner together.
- Host sleepovers with close friends.
- Go on playdates.

Making Memories for us is about traveling together and having shared adventures. We had ideas all over the place here, all the way from a vacation in Australia to having weekend adventures close to home.

Honoring Commitments is about holding each other accountable to our family systems. We had things like doing our weekly family meetings and totaling our S.T.A.R.R. charts daily.

Genuine Contribution is about giving back as a family. We had ideas to raise money for charity for each of our birthdays instead of receiving gifts and volunteer as a family.

Financial Literacy is about teaching the kids some money concepts. Some of our ideas included investing money in stocks, reviewing them monthly, and listening to a book about money together.

Now that we had several ideas in each category, it was time to narrow them down to be specific, measurable, achievable, realistic, and time-bound. For example, we had lots of different exercises for healthy habits. We asked the kids what *done* would look like? We thought the easiest way was to exercise together as a family forty times per year. That is a little less than once a week, which we thought was both realistic and achievable. It's also specific, measurable, and time-bound. Another example is in honoring commitments; we wanted to have weekly family meetings. There are fifty-two weeks in a year, but we also travel a lot, so we decided forty family meetings for the year was realistic. We went through each idea in the same way to make them all specific, measurable, achievable, realistic, and time-bound. When we finished, we put them all into a Google Sheet, so we could track them easily. During our weekly family meetings, we update our spreadsheet for the week.

Each person also set two major goals for the year, one hard one and one fun one. Ember's hard goal was to learn to read, and her fun one was to learn to jump on a horse. Tyler set his hard goal to finish level six at school, and his fun goal was to land a kickflip on a skateboard. Mike's hard goal was to achieve optimal health, and his fun goal was to be in total alignment with his spirit. My hard goal was to launch this book, and my fun goal was to have a monthly girl's night out with friends. These are not necessarily "S.M.A.R.T.E.R." goals, but each week during our family meeting, we have the kids set weekly goals with these in mind.

WHAT DOES THE FINISHED PRODUCT LOOK LIKE?

The following chart is from June, which is about the time we'd evaluate and readjust based on the percentages. You will notice, there are a few that are zeros. Those are the categories to start with and figure out why they are zeros. For cooking dinner together, we discovered it's not something we like doing together very much. I like to cook, and having the kids in the kitchen slows me down. The kids love to help me bake, and they often make their meals now that they are older, so we will probably take that goal out.

Another goal was for the kids to eat what we eat. That one is probably not as achievable as we anticipated. Tyler is vegetarian, and Ember is not, so there are very few meals that the entire family will eat. The ones we will all eat are not the healthiest options, so that goal, too, probably needs to be removed.

We have a zero for hiking a 14er together, but that is a summer-only activity, so it could still be achieved. We also haven't read a money book together, but we still have time. For the rest, we would look to see if there is still enough time in the year to reach them; if so, we're all good. If not, we need to adjust the number so it's realistic. One goal, we are crushing and already have 216% halfway through the year. That number needs to be adjusted too. Here is what our spreadsheet looks like. We also have a tracking page with more specific details that feed the totals of this page.

Family Goals			
Authentic Relationships	**Goal**	**Actual**	**% Complete**
Family Board Meetings	24	14	58.33%
Game Nights	40	12	30.00%
Cook dinner together	40	0	0.00%
Family Movie Night	40	11	27.50%
Facetime Grandparents (1 x Month each)	36	8	22.22%
Read/Listen Same Book	10	3	30.00%
Genuine Contribution	**Goal**	**Actual**	**% Complete**
Launch a Kids Business	1	1	100.00%
Donate Birthday to Charity	4	2	50.00%
Attend Church / Spiritual Center	6	13	216.67%
Healthy Habits	**Goal**	**Actual**	**% Complete**
Family Exercise	40	24	60.00%
Kids eat what we eat	40	0	0.00%
Preventative Dr. Visits	3	2	66.67%
Honoring Commitments	**Goal**	**Actual**	**% Complete**
Family Dream Sessions	40	17	42.50%
Track Weekly Star Totaling	40	15	37.50%
Bucket List Adventures	**Goal**	**Actual**	**% Complete**
Solo Family Trip	1	1	100.00%
10 Weekend Trips	10	4	40.00%
4 National Parks	4	3	75.00%
Camping Trips	3	2	66.67%
GoPod Family Trip	1	1	100.00%
Hike a 14er Together	1	1	0.00%
Financial Literacy	**Goal**	**Actual**	**% Complete**
Invest Money review monthly	12	8	66.67%
Read Money Book as a Family	1	0	0.00%

—YOUR TURN—
CREATE YOUR FAMILY GOALS

SUPPLIES:

- Your family
- Family Goals Worksheet or paper—one sheet per person (you can download additional copies of the worksheet from www.miraclemorning.com/parentsplaybook)
- Something to write with—one per person
- Optional: computer to type up a spreadsheet

OBJECTIVE:

The objective of this exercise is to set goals as a family, modeling the process of setting individual goals for your kids.

THIS EXERCISE HAS SIX STEPS:

1. Set individual big goals.
2. Decide on categories.
3. Generate ideas.
4. Consolidate ideas and make them S.M.A.R.T.
5. Set up spreadsheet and track.
6. Evaluate and readjust.

STEP ONE: SET INDIVIDUAL BIG GOALS.

Work with each family member to come up with two big personal goals. Pick one goal that is hard and one goal that is fun. These are big goals that each person is committed to working toward over a longer period of time—six months to a year.

STEP TWO: DECIDE ON CATEGORIES.

We used the categories from GoBundance since we are familiar with them, but you can use any categories you see fit for your family. If you'd like to borrow our categories, here they are again: Healthy Habits, Authentic Relationships, Making Memories, Honoring Commitments, Genuine Contribution, and Financial Literacy. You could also use your family values as the categories for setting your goals.

STEP THREE: GENERATE IDEAS.

Go through each of the categories you've set and come up with as many goal ideas as you can for each. Remember, the idea here is to generate lots of ideas. Don't edit them now; that will come in the next step.

STEP FOUR: CONSOLIDATE IDEAS AND MAKE THEM S.M.A.R.T.

This is the time to pare the goal ideas down, decide what's most important, and make the goals specific, measurable, achievable, relevant, and time-bound. To help with this step, you can ask the following questions: What would *done* look like? How much can we realistically fit in this year, month, week? Does this goal line up with our values? For each goal category, set one to five goals.

STEP FIVE: SET UP A SPREADSHEET AND TRACK.

This step is optional, but we have found it is the easiest way for us to stay consistent with tracking. I prefer to make two Google Sheets. The first is like you saw above, which has the bottom-line goals with totals and percent complete. The other is a tracking sheet with more specifics.

For example, we have a goal to read ten books as a family this year. On the first sheet, it just lists the goal, actual, and percentage. On the second sheet, there would be a place for book title, date finished, and a place to total the number of books read. I would then copy and paste the total from the second sheet to the first sheet in the "actual" column. That way, it will auto-populate that spot when I update the tracking sheet.

STEP SIX: EVALUATE AND READJUST.

You may want to do this quarterly or mid-year. Take a look at your numbers and see if there are any goals that aren't S.M.A.R.T. There are many reasons a goal might be off track. Maybe it wasn't aligned with your values, maybe it was an ideal but not realistic in practice, maybe someone in the family got sick, and their health became the top priority in the family. This is not a time to point fingers and blame, but a time to take a hard look at the goals and readjust to make them more doable. There's no shame in taking a goal off the list or readjusting to a lower number to make it achievable.

FAMILY GOALS WORKSHEET

STEP ONE: SET INDIVIDUAL BIG GOALS.

Work with each family member to come up with two big personal goals. Pick one goal that is hard and one goal that is fun. These are big goals that each person is committed to working toward over a longer period of time—six months to one year.

My Big HARD Goal for the year is to:: _____

My Big FUN Goal for the year is to: _____

STEP TWO: DECIDE ON CATEGORIES.

What are the categories that are most important for your family to set goals in?

_____

_____

STEP THREE: GENERATE IDEAS.

Go through each of the categories you've set and come up with as many goal ideas as you can for each.

_____

_____

STEP FOUR: CONSOLIDATE IDEAS AND MAKE THEM S.M.A.R.T.

This is the time to pare the goal ideas down, decide what's most important, and make the goals specific, measurable, achievable, relevant, and time-bound. For each goal category, set one to five goals.

_____

_____

EXERCISE SEVEN: YOUR FAMILY MEETING

"Teach me and I'll forget. Show me and I may remember. Involve me and I will learn."

—Benjamin Franklin, American Founding Father

WHY IS IT IMPORTANT?

We can't overstate the importance of having dedicated space and time to consistently get on the same page as a family, lift up our values, express gratitude, support each other in achieving goals, and have conversations around what's important as a family. If you're a business owner, you probably meet with key employees regularly to stay on the same page, so why not do it with your family too? It's a super practical way to plan for the week ahead and get everyone in the family involved. We believe children also learn so much during these meetings, including good listening skills, problem-solving, respecting others' opinions, verbalizing ideas, the power of family values, goal setting, expressing gratitude, effective collaboration, and scheduling priorities. They are also a great opportunity to create family traditions and memories.

One family meeting that always stands out to me is the day we had to say goodbye to our Rottweiler, Stella. On a Sunday morning, it was clear she was in a lot of pain. We took her to the emergency vet and had to make the heart-wrenching decision to put her down.

We had planned to do a family meeting that day, and Mike and I debated if we still should. We decided that we would still do it, but we altered it to be all about Stella. We had the kids share some of their favorite memories of her, and we all shared our gratitude about what a great dog she was for our family.

We also talked about how we could honor her in the future to keep her memory alive. We decided to make October 21 "Stella Day." We would celebrate by watching movies about dogs together and decided to make a photo book to remember her.

We spent the rest of the day snuggled up on the couch together, watching movies about dogs. That family meeting turned a really difficult day into a time of family connection.

HOW DID WE DO IT?

We started having family meetings to create the systems in this book. Once they were all up and running, we wanted to come together regularly to go over some details about life, have a protected time to manage these systems, and be able to discuss and make any changes as a family.

The first thing we needed to decide was what we were going to call it. Everyone knows meetings are boring, even kids, so we didn't want to call it that. To us, it was a time to dream about the future and then make it into reality, so we decided to call ours The McCarthy Family Dream Session.

We also needed to decide the frequency of our dream sessions. We decided to aim for once a week. We picked a morning on the weekend since we're usually available during that time.

Next came the fun part and lots of experimenting. We had to decide what was going to be on the agenda for our weekly Family Dream Session. We had lots of ideas that ranged from practical to frivolous. Some of the ideas were to share gratitude and high-point moments to celebrate our peak experiences, go over the schedule for the week, count down to our next family adventure or holiday, review family values and goals, track financials, learn financial lessons, review stocks, plan our next adventures, talk about important issues that came up during the week, update any family systems that need tweaking, create a meal plan, review weekly S.T.A.R.R. chart results, or even have a family dance party or special handshake to close.

Once we had lots of ideas, it was time to pare them down so the Family Dream Session wouldn't take all day. We liked the idea of starting the meeting with gratitude to help shift our focus to the positive. Sharing high-point moments and reviewing our peak experiences also made the cut.

Humans have a pretty bad memory, but when you recall something right before you forget it, that memory moves to your long-term memory and becomes easier to hold on to.

One of the main reasons for our Family Dream Session is to purposefully pass on our family values to our kids, so we thought it would be a good idea to recite our values together at each Dream Session.

We also wanted to guide our kids toward setting goals and model that behavior for them, so we included that too. From a practical standpoint, going over the schedule for the week in the context of our overall goals made a lot of sense in keeping everyone on the same page.

Those five became the essentials: gratitude, high points, family values, schedule, and goals. After that, we left it open-ended. Anyone could bring up any issue they wanted to discuss. If there was a problem with the S.T.A.R.R. chart, that was the time to discuss it. If someone thought a rule on the screen-time contract was unfair, that was the time to bring it up. If someone wanted to make a suggestion for dinner that week, that was the time to make the suggestion. This is not to say that we do not discuss these things outside our Family Dream Sessions, but it's a safe space when the whole family is present to make a decision.

We like to have closure to the session, so when everything is done, we all put our hands in the middle, count to three, and shout, "McCarthys!"

These meetings do not happen *every* week in our household. We follow the rule that it's okay to skip one week, but never two in a row. Even if it's a condensed session, it's better than no meeting at all. The weeks we don't get everyone together on the weekend, we often feel flustered. We don't have the same focus we normally have, and those are typically the times when the most miscommunications happen. It is certainly in our best interest to stay consistent.

WHAT DOES THE FINISHED PRODUCT LOOK LIKE?

MCCARTHY FAMILY DREAM SESSION AGENDA

1. START WITH GRATITUDE.

Everyone should start by writing or drawing one thing they're grateful for in general—it doesn't have to be family related.

Then write down why you are grateful for each member of your family, and don't forget yourself. Some great things to include are which family value you saw them living or how they helped you this week.

Example: I am grateful for Mike for being a resilient warrior this week, driving the camper van over 1,000 miles without cruise control.

Next, everyone picks a family member and goes around the circle, doing a round of shares, showering that person with love and gratitude! Repeat this step for everyone in the family. Whoever goes first will share what they are grateful for in general, then everyone will share why they are grateful for that person, ending with them sharing why they are grateful for themselves before moving on to the next family member.

Example: If Ember goes first, she will share why she is grateful in general, then Tyler will share why he's grateful for his sister, Mom will share why she's grateful for her daughter, Dad will share why he's grateful for his daughter, and Ember will finish with why she is grateful for herself. Then, we move on to Tyler and repeat until everyone has been showered with love.

2. SHARE HIGH-POINT MOMENTS FROM THE WEEK.

Think about your best moments from this past week, both for yourself and together as a family.

Everyone should write or draw them in their journal. Some examples of this are funny moments, activities you did together, challenges you overcame, or anything else you can think of that really made your week!

Go around the circle and share your moments.

3. RECITE FAMILY VALUES.

Read your family values aloud, one at a time, and have the rest of the family repeat them back to the reader.

4. REVIEW GOALS.

For this step, we'll be focusing on two areas: our one to three biggest goals for the year, as well as our small weekly goals.

Big Goals: Start by going around in a circle and checking in on your one to three big goals for the year and where you currently stand in achieving them. This could also be an opportunity to update these goals, especially if you happen to accomplish them early.

Weekly Goals: What were your weekly goals from last week? How did you do? What other goals do you need to set for the week ahead, both that will help you to achieve your big goals and others that will help you have a great week.

Family Goals: Look at the goals you've set as a family. If you have a tracking page, this is a great time to update it. Also, as you go over the schedule for the week in the next step, find some spots to schedule in your family goals.

5. SCHEDULE THE WEEK.

Go over the schedule for the next week, day by day, for each member of the family. If you have time, you can look further ahead on the calendar and plan for your next family adventure or fill in some time to accomplish family goals.

6. COVER ANYTHING ELSE.

This is the time to bring up anything else that has come up during the week or to review any family systems that need tweaking.

Once a month, we check the kid's stocks and update a spreadsheet so they can see how they have done over time.

7. CLOSE.

Now that everyone is on the same page, it's time to celebrate. Everyone put your hands in. One, two, three, McCarthys!

If you find yourself shouting, "McCarthys!" at *your* family meeting, you might want to reassess.

—YOUR TURN—
CREATE YOUR FAMILY MEETING AGENDA

SUPPLIES:

- Your family
- The Family Meeting Agenda Worksheet (you can download additional copies of this worksheet from www.miraclemorning.com/parentsplaybook)
- Easel, whiteboard, or wall
- Sticky notes
- Pencils, pens, or markers
- For future meetings, it's helpful for each person to have a dedicated "family meeting" journal

OBJECTIVE:

The objective of this exercise is to create an agenda for your regular family meeting.

THIS EXERCISE HAS FIVE STEPS:

1. Generate ideas.
2. Share ideas.
3. Discuss and pare down ideas.
4. Write up agenda and schedule next meeting.
5. Close out the meeting.

STEP ONE: GENERATE IDEAS.

Set a timer for ten minutes, and write down as many ideas as you can that answer the following questions: How often should our family meet to get on the same page? What might our family connect about on a weekly, biweekly, or monthly basis? What should we call our family meetings?

What are some areas we need to all be on the same page with as a family? What would be a fun way to close each meeting? Write or draw one idea per sticky note. Here are some ideas to get you started: schedules, goals, family values, gratitude, high-point moments, etc.

STEP TWO: SHARE IDEAS.

Now, it's time to share your ideas. Go around the circle, having each person share one idea at a time, capture each idea on a sticky note, and place it on the easel. Repeat this process until all ideas are on the easel. If you had the same idea, go ahead and add it to the board when it's shared. If the same idea came from two different people, you know the idea has energy behind it. Remember, this is the step to generate ideas. All ideas should be accepted without discussion. You will pare them down in the next step.

STEP THREE: DISCUSS AND PARE DOWN IDEAS.

Now that all the ideas have been shared, it's time to talk about the ideas and make some decisions. If there was an idea that multiple family members had in common, that is probably a good indication you should keep it. By the end of this step, you should have decided how often your family is committed to meeting, what you will call your family meeting, your key agenda items, and your closing ritual. In our experience, once you get past five to seven agenda items, it is harder to manage time-wise, so keep that in mind.

If you struggle to come together in this step, you may want to start with just one agenda item and build up from there. A good focus question is: What's the *one* thing we might discuss regularly that would help our family get on the same page?" Commit to meeting every week to talk about that one thing, and once it has become a habit, you can add more agenda items.

STEP FOUR: WRITE UP AN AGENDA AND SCHEDULE THE NEXT MEETING.

It's time to put it all together. Have one person in the family write out your agenda for your first family meeting. Make sure you schedule one on the calendar before you close this meeting.

STEP FIVE: CLOSE OUT THE MEETING.

Take a moment right now and end this exercise by practicing your closing ritual as a family. It's important to have a ritual to close the meeting, so everyone knows the meeting is over, such as a family chant, an empowering saying, a family hug, or a ritual like all putting your hands in and saying the family name with enthusiasm. Sometimes, sensitive topics come up, and emotions can run high. We've found having a closing to the meeting at least brings everyone together at the end.

FAMILY MEETING AGENDA WORKSHEET

STEP ONE: GENERATE IDEAS.

Set a timer for ten minutes, and write down as many ideas as you can to answer the following questions:

1. How often should our family meet to get on the same page?

2. What might our family connect about on a weekly, biweekly, or monthly basis?

3. What should we call our family meetings?

4. What are some areas we need to all be on the same page as a family?

5. What would be a fun way to close each meeting? Write or draw one idea per sticky note. Here are some ideas to get you started: schedules, goals, family values, gratitude, high-point moments, etc.

STEP TWO: SHARE IDEAS.

Now it's time to share your ideas. Go around the circle, having each person share one idea at a time, capture each idea on a sticky note, and place it on the easel. Repeat this process until all ideas are on the easel.

STEP THREE: DISCUSS AND PARE DOWN IDEAS.

Now that all the ideas have been shared, it's time to talk about the ideas and make some decisions. If there was an idea that multiple family members had in common, that is probably a good indication you should keep it.

How often is your family committed to meeting? _____

What will you call your family meeting? _____

What are the five to seven key agenda items you will discuss at each meeting?

1. _____
2. _____
3. _____
4. _____
5. _____
6. _____
7. _____

What is your family's closing ritual for the end of meetings? _____

FINAL THOUGHTS

We hope this playbook helped you create some of your own family systems, values, goals, and rhythms. It took us years to get all of these in place in our household.

As they become habits, the checklists will become a thing of the past.

As your values become ingrained, they become guideposts for your family.

We wrote this book to guide other families to create healthy habits and boundaries in their households the same way we did in ours. We do not think we are perfect parents or that we have it all figured out. We are still learning and growing all the time, but if this book can help even one family create more harmony and togetherness in their home, then it was worth it.

ABOUT THE AUTHORS

Mike and Lindsay McCarthy have been married for fifteen years and have two amazing children, Tyler (twelve) and Ember (eight). They live in Austin, Texas, but spend some time in the summer and winter at their home in Silverthorne, Colorado. The McCarthys are an active family and love to be outdoors hiking, biking, skiing, snowboarding, skating, kayaking, paddleboarding, or walking their Beagle, Bodhi. Their new family obsession is traveling around the country in their "Adventure Mobile."

Mike is the regional owner for the Greater Pennsylvania region of Keller Williams Realty, Xchange facilitator and cofounder of GoBundance, and coauthor of *The Miracle Morning for Parents and Families* and *Tribe of Millionaires*.

Lindsay is mainly a stay-at-home mom and occasionally writes blogs on their website, GratefulParent.com, and runs the Facebook Community for *The Miracle Morning for Parents and Families*.

ACKNOWLEDGMENTS

First and foremost, we want to thank our friends, the Elrods. Hal says, "Sometimes you need someone else to believe in you before you can believe in yourself." He believed we could write a book before we did and gave us the amazing opportunity to fulfill that dream in such a big way with *The Miracle Morning for Parents and Families*. We're grateful for your friendship and that we could partner with you again for this project. Ursula, thanks for being a great friend and neighbor. We will miss having you right down the street but love that we still get to do life together.

We also want to thank our children, Tyler and Ember, for being our guinea pigs. Thank you for showing up for our Family Dream Sessions and helping us cocreate our family values and systems. Thanks for making us parents and for the joy you've brought to our lives. Thank you for being our teachers and always keeping us on our toes. We love you so much and can't wait to see what the future holds for you both.

A big thank you to our FamBundance family. We love you guys! Thank you for showing up to our events and helping build an amazing village for all our kids to grow up in. Thank you to Brotha James for providing us with your musical talents and facilitating skills. Braden DeLonay, we appreciate your calming nature and your willingness to jump in and help out wherever we need you. Thanks to Matt Duncan for helping with the kids' programming and creating a lot of our early worksheets. Thanks to Jon Berghoff for training all our facilitators and sharing the power of Appreciative Inquiry through the Xchange program. Thanks to Cecil Cummings and all the other GoCrew we've had at our events; we couldn't have done them without you. Thanks to Jeff Tucker and his team at Tucker Media for capturing our events over the years. Special thanks to all the speakers and guests we've had at our events, especially Jim and Jamie Sheils, Jon Vroman, Karen Delano, Nick Santanantasso, Hal Elrod, Aaron Velky, McClain Hermes, David Osborn, Charlie Engle, Kim Hess, Solomon Masala and Wendy and Jay Papasan.

I (Lindsay) would like to thank Brianna Greenspan for giving me the push I needed to write this book and Amanda Rooker at Split Seed Media for helping me get it off the ground and organized. Thank you to The Miracle Morning team for helping with all the things we have no idea how to do. Honorée Corder, thank you for coordinating all the things and lining up the talent to create the cover, edit the book, and get it out to the world. Tiffany Hammond, thank you for all your work behind the scenes. You ladies rock!

Made in the USA
Middletown, DE
19 November 2021

52906822R00053